GOD
GRACE
AND
HORSES

GOD GRACE AND HORSES

Life Lessons from the Saddle

LAURIE M. BROCK

PARACLETE PRESS
BREWSTER, MASSACHUSETTS

2022 First Printing

God, Grace, and Horses: Life Lessons from the Saddle

Copyright © 2022 by Laurie M. Brock

ISBN 978-1-64060-607-4

Unless otherwise noted, the Scripture quotations contained herein are from the New Revised Standard Version Bible, copyright © 1989 by the Division of Christian Education of the National Council of Churches of Christ in the U.S.A. Used by permission. All rights reserved.

The Paraclete Press name and logo (dove on cross) are trademarks of Paraclete Press.

   Library of Congress Cataloging-in-Publication Data
Names: Brock, Laurie M., 1968- author.
Title: God, grace, and horses : life lessons from the saddle / Laurie M.
  Brock.
Description: Brewster : Paraclete Press, 2021. | Summary: "Episcopal priest
  and horse-lover Laurie Brock explores the holy trails where only horses
  can take us, and where God walks with us"– Provided by publisher.
Identifiers: LCCN 2021036479 | ISBN 9781640606074 (trade paperback) | ISBN
  9781640606081 (epub) | ISBN 9781640606098 (pdf)
Subjects: LCSH: Horses–Religious aspects–Christianity. |
  Spirituality–Christianity.
Classification: LCC BV4596.A54 B76 2021 | DDC 248.2/9–dc23
LC record available at https://lccn.loc.gov/2021036479

10 9 8 7 6 5 4 3 2 1

Published by Paraclete Press
Brewster, Massachusetts
www.paracletepress.com

Printed in the United States of America

To
THE WEDNESDAY NIGHT RIDERS
at Wingswept Farm.

And in memory of
CHAMPION TIPITINA,
who let us soar when we rode her.

And of
JACK,
who taught so many to love horses.
Your love and spirit remain with us.

And to
NINA,
always.

CONTENTS

INTRODUCTION

*H*umans walk about four miles an hour. When we lived in a time when walking was our main mode of movement, our lives and our communities were fairly small—our entire world probably existed about ten or twenty miles around us.

I'm not sure, for most of us, our daily lives today exist much beyond that same ten or twenty miles, but the possibility, even the probability, of more, is attainable and fairly effortless. We drive our cars to the new restaurant in the next town over on a Friday night. We catch a train to move across several states in a few hours. We board a plane and go across the country or the world for a business trip or vacation. We journey and move to new places without much thought.

Our ancestors moved differently. They walked. If they were ingenious and daring and near a body of water that wasn't too deadly to navigate, they boated.

Until the horse.

That one partnership, that one moment when one creature of God looked at another creature of God and wondered, "What if?" changed us. Humans formed a relationship with something that moved us beyond the known and familiar. While humans and horses walk about the same speed, horses can trot long distances at eight miles per hour and gallop at up to thirty-five miles per hour for short distances. A well-conditioned horse can cover one hundred miles per day.

Our relationship with horses moved us beyond the world we knew into something larger and vaster. Horses gave us the ability to explore, to connect with other peoples and communities, and to move differently. Suddenly a village that was two hours away by walking on our own two feet became easily accessible on horseback. Horses connected us with each other, just by their very embodiment, by doing what horses do.

And horses did something else. We could take things with us. A person used to carrying things from place to place can generously carry forty to fifty pounds. A horse, however, can carry about 200 pounds. Add a cart to that, and now that same horse can transport twice their body weight. So that village two hours away by foot suddenly becomes closer, and now we can take things.

We could also use the strength of a horse to plow fields and grow more food. And horses became our partners in defending our communities from those who were not welcome or, perhaps unfortunately, offered us ways to invade other communities. Trade, interaction, community, and even our modern concepts of political societies began to take shape in a new way. Because of horses.

Not until the early 1800s did the advent of steam locomotion have such a tremendous impact on how humans move in our daily lives. But we've been in a relationship with horses for around 6,000 years.

My relationship with horses began when I was three. My father's family had horses, and one of my first times sitting on a horse was captured in a photograph. When I see it, I see two creatures of God who are wondering, "What if?" What if I rode you to somewhere else? What if I listened to your wisdom, to who you are? What if my breath became so intertwined with yours that I learned to breathe better, to live better, to pray better? What if I let you move me in a different way to an understanding of God and grace that was beyond anything I could discover on my own?

I'm still trying to do these things.

However, I'm fairly sure my three-year-old self didn't think any of that, not then. I just loved holding on to the thick, wavy mane of the mare on which I sat.

I rode casually and inconsistently for years until my soul needed to be moved away from the familiarity I had known, the ten- to twenty-mile radius of the words of the prayers of faith I'd used, still holy and useful, until my soul knew that just over the edge of the landscape, God had something . . . more.

And the one way I could get there involved a horse.

So I saddled up and rode. I got some bruises and broken bones along the way. I shed some tears in the face of the overwhelming feeling that is stepping into something new for the first time, or stepping into something new for the seven hundredth time but realizing that on this occasion the journey will forever mark your soul. You may not even be aware that you're on such a journey until you are well down the road.

The Kentucky cowgirl in me was excited about this journey. She is always up for any excuse to wear her boots. But the priest who spent more time than she often wanted in the margins of mystery and vulnerability of human life, felt a bit of dread and absurdity about an adventure that guaranteed a shift, a transformation, a difference, a movement somewhere. But the human in me? She took a deep breath and climbed in the saddle.

Kentucky writer Wendell Berry shares this ambivalence, when we leave the familiar, secure places and venture into unknown wide-open spaces: "You are undertaking the first experience, not of the place, but of yourself in that place. It is an experience of our essential loneliness, for nobody can discover the world for anybody else."[1]

Humans have ridden horses for eons, and we've been in a relationship with them for far longer. These chapters are all about my experience in the saddle. No other human can discover the world for anybody else, but we can resonate with each other's experiences. We can and do need companions along the way as we learn to move differently. I saddled up, and let horses move me from what was familiar into what I needed to discover about God, about grace, and about me.

GOD
GRACE
AND
HORSES

PART ONE
ON THE TRAIL

The spiritual journey is like a road
that goes from somewhere to nowhere.
We know the starting point, but we see the destination only dimly.
—MICHAEL CASEY, *GRACE: ON THE JOURNEY TO GOD*

I balanced on the second rail of the fence and pulled my left leg over the top rail. Checking the ground on the other side to make sure it wasn't a slop of spring mud, I made the short jump down to the ground. Jumping over a fence was one of those significant measures of age—it is a skill that gets more challenging as the birthdays pass, as my knees reminded me when I landed.

Tonight, I was jumping a fence into the field where the pregnant mares were grazing. A large piece of white plastic had blown into the field. Some of the mares were already wary of this interloper into their paddock. Horses, for all their vast, deep intelligence, also have the amazing ability to find trouble. My grandfather once noted that if you had one hundred acres fenced off for a horse to live in with one nail sticking out of one board on that long line of fence, a horse will find the one nail on the one board and manage to hurt itself.

This six-foot piece of plastic would certainly be terrifying enough to startle the mares, and they did not need to be startled with babies so close to being born. Some of the mares eyed me, the new interloper in their space. They quickly went back to grazing. Apparently, I didn't register as a threat to them.

I wadded up the white plastic and climbed back on the fence, taking some time to sit on the weathered wooden rail in the March evening, a bit warmer than usual. After several weeks of March's leonine ice storms, snowfall, and lows well below zero, I appreciated the toasty evening in the high forty-degree range. I watched this group of mares, their bellies lush and heavy in various stages of carrying the newest generation of Wingswept foals. After several moments, two of them began to walk on the trail they had made.

In this field, one of the larger ones at Wingswept Farm, where I ride horses in the Bluegrass region of Kentucky, the horses have walked in the same steps as horses from years past and created a well-trodden series of trails in this field. They have a huge spread of grass, but a three-foot packed dirt ribbon looped over the hill from the front part of the field and meandered down to where I now sat on the fence. The path branched, and the branches led to a water trough, their feed buckets, and the run-in shed, which is a three-sided building open in the front so horses can run into it and be sheltered from the weather. These are the common places all horses need to find to survive.

We humans follow trails to the place we need to find to survive, although I'm not sure we're as efficient as horses are. I'm certainly not.

I've followed plenty of trails I didn't carve out, or really even want to walk. But when I was young, when we are all young, part of youth is following the trails created by those who are older and presumably wiser (although not always). I've wandered over many trails, hoping they would lead somewhere, to something I needed to survive. Some did. Many didn't.

I walked a trail away from the faith of my childhood and youth that didn't lead to a place of springs. It led instead into the wilderness of believing in God, but not believing in a formal religion. That path was wide-open, and I needed to wander for quite some time. Then I listened to a quiet whisper that invited me down another trail to find the Episcopal Church, and eventually another trail to ordination. Those trails were well-trod and well-packed by the many who walked them before me, but God still called me, as God calls all of us, to walk our own way.

I walked the manicured trails and followed the arrows and again found myself following the trails marked by others. These trails were often the trails of "supposed to" and career advancement. Yes, even in the church, we speak of decisions and choices that will look good on the resume. Clergy often gave me advice how I, as a young woman priest, could be taken "more seriously" as a priest. So once again, I found myself too often going from one destination to another, following the directions of others because I was fearful of wandering, fearful of being lost, fearful of following the trails God called me on that might not be as well-worn or as clearly marked.

One evening, while preparing for a Sunday school class I was teaching, I wondered just how far the Hebrews actually had to walk from Egypt to the Promised Land. I dragged out my Bible atlas, which had been mostly unused since seminary. I discovered that the distance, about 240 miles on the most direct route, meant that the Israelites basically averaged six miles per year on their journey.

Even if they were taking a leisurely stroll and in no hurry to settle down in a homeland, six miles per year seems to be an incredibly slow pace, a pace that is almost purposeful in its dawdling. Using the average human and horse walking speed of three to four miles per hour, walking four hours a day for five days a week, the Hebrews would have arrived in the Promised Land in about a month.

And yet, they didn't.

Something about wandering in the desert for forty years mattered, and that wandering formed them into the chosen people of God who were embraced in covenant.

Being the people of God is not something we earn; it is instead a space we inhabit not from our sureness, but from our vulnerability and wandering and learning, of walking on trails that lead to somewhere and some that lead to nowhere. This forming came and comes from experiencing things vastly different from our expectations, from a fair amount of complaining and arguing (WHEN are we getting there?!?), from obedience and disobedience, with consequences for both.

I had slipped into the patterns of following trails because someone else suggested them, rather than doing my own work and discernment to follow the trail God called me to walk. The many trails we encounter can be confusing, to say the least. Not all of them lead to things that are life-giving.

I shifted on the fence and watched a group of mares follow the trail from the far edge of the field to the run-in shed. Night was coming and my guess was that they sensed the winter wind was not done on this March evening and would be arriving in the next few hours. Horses are sometimes better predictors of weather than the local news.

They also know how to follow a trail. Whether from smell or memory or a combination of senses, horses can find their way to where they need to go. For those of us who join them for the ride, they take us where we need to go too.

Almost a decade ago, when I found myself on the trail of working too much and having too little of a life that fed me with the sustenance of God, quenched my thirst for love, and sheltered me when I was vulnerable, I found horses. I followed an unlikely trail to them, and horses took me on another trail, a holy trail.

Most of the trails I ride with them have been walked before. Sometimes we wander in the meadows behind the barn. Sometimes I find trails in wide-open spaces on new horses.

Being on the trail with horses gives me space to breathe and to be.

They notice things, and I notice things.

They are companions along the way, to sometimes ask me if this indeed is the trail we need to take. They slow me down when I feel rushed, their meandering walking pace giving my soul time to catch up with my body.

Horses take me on the holy trails where God walks with us.

CHAPTER 1
Easy Silence

❧

For God alone my soul in silence waits;
truly, here is my hope.
—PSALM 62:6 [2]

*C*entering prayer is a prayer practice that involves silence, an emptying almost, of our words and even images as we offer ourselves in prayer with God simply by our presence. Practitioners sit for a significant time, finding silent union with God. The method I was taught involves choosing a word to center my intention, and when my thoughts drift away from the simple silence that is the pure encounter with God, the word serves as a way back to the place of prayer. Cistercian monk Thomas Keating is credited with bringing centering prayer into the common practice of many Christians. A Buddhist monk colleague opined that it resembled the meditation practice some Buddhists have practiced for a few eons.

I didn't disagree.

She invited me to practice meditation with her, and some months ago I decided I needed to amp up my prayer practice and agreed to join her once a week.

Why? Who knows. In a moment of searching for things that will make the hard questions and the hardness of life easier, I thought sitting in quiet contemplation would be the answer. Emptying myself to the fullness of God would give me a way to connect with God. I've always admired my friends who practiced centering prayer each day. Centering prayer seemed a level up from the Daily Office I prayed each morning and evening. Advanced prayer, I guess.

In our first session, she invited me to sit comfortably in a cross-legged position and blow my nose as we began our practice of meditation/centering prayer. Cleaning out one's nostrils is apparently a good precursor to prayer. We started.

I shifted.

She sat.

I shifted and found myself wondering about the sale that started at the tack store tomorrow. I could always use a new pair of riding boots.

As if she could read my mind, she said, "Draw your awareness back to your breath, not to the distractions of the day."

I breathed, but rather than a release into God kind of breath, it was more like one of those exasperated sighs that my horse, Nina, gives me when I have given her the last of the peppermints and now she's forced to eat her hay.

I made it for five practices, my frustration growing with each one. I've always been an advocate that committing to a daily prayer practice takes work. After all, the ancestors of my faith didn't call it a spiritual discipline for nothing. Discipline is work. Discipline reminds us that there are tasks necessary for instruction and learning that aren't easy or fun. For me, this prayer practice felt like I was praying to get myself out of trouble, as if I had to write, "I will sit in profound silence to find God," on the chalkboard one thousand times or be banished to the outer darkness where there is weeping and gnashing of teeth.

Prayer as penitential chastisement is apparently a bridge too far for my soul, so on the day I had my sixth meditation practice on my calendar, I texted my Buddhist colleague that I deeply appreciated her time, but after reflection, I realized I was not experiencing God in this type of sitting prayer, and I needed a few weeks' break.

Actually, I texted that something came up at the church and I'd talk to her later.

I'm a born explainer, thinking somehow if I flesh out the reason I don't like something, the perceived rejection will land more softly. However, the part of me that has slowly learned that "No" is a complete sentence stepped outside on this perfect spring day and said, "Let's go ride."

Which is exactly what I did.

I went to the barn, saddled up Nina—my elegant, sassy princess, a chestnut-colored American Saddlebred horse—and set off for a ride on the paths that surround the barn in the woods.

Kentucky has four distinct seasons, sometimes all in one day. The stagnant heat of summer was still months away, and the icy exhaustion of winter had finally given way to spring. Spring had secured its presence, which in Kentucky is no small feat. From the last snowfall until the sustained arrival of spring, we can have any number of winters, all with a name—redbud winter, dogwood winter, locust winter, blackberry winter, and linsey-woolsey britches winter. The last one usually arrives in late May and is the final appearance of winter clothing made of a homespun linen-wool combination. Or, by today's standards, the Patagonia puffer jacket winter, which had come and gone two weeks ago.

Spring is the season where all creation stretches and moves again, freed from the deep rest winter demands and, in fact, our souls demand. We need rest, the deep repose that winter offers in the more northern climates. My ancestors spent winter by pot-bellied stoves mending clothes and sitting. Of course, animals needed to be fed and wood needed to be chopped, but winter was by and large a time of lying fallow.

Then, slowly, days lengthened and snow melted, leaving mud. Lots of mud. I kept a pair of muck boots in my SUV for the trudge into a paddock to get a horse or the walk to the barn. There, I changed into old riding boots, saddled up Nina, and let her stomp through the mud to the trail, less muddy because the roots of trees rousing from their winter rest were taking the water into themselves and flinging it out in spurts of green leaves and white, red, pink, and purple blossoms.

The air was warm with just enough bits of chill to keep the sweat from running down my back and the bugs at bay. I clucked Nina forward past the edge of the fence line. We walked past the paddock where Woody the stallion, whom she hates, lived, and then moved through a gateway of dogwood branches into the easy silence of the woods.

A few feet in and Nina realized we were on a trail ride. Nina thinks trail rides are the cat's pajamas. Her ears pricked up, her hind hooves pranced. She was excited.

In response to her energy, I sank into her. My hips rolled under slightly and my rear sat deeply in the saddle. I got comfortable and quiet. My feet dropped out of the stirrups and my legs reached downward, letting gravity gently add space between bones and joints that are too often pounded into each other by the jarring work of living.

Being with her energy allowed me to rest in my lack of it. In these moments on the trail, I don't have to be up or ready. I'm not worried about my shoulders being back or holding her head in that position that stretches her neck out in an elegant arch, which are the hallmarks of riding a Saddlebred. We were on a trail, and the audience was simply each other. I became part of her for the time I was on the trail and could simply ride. I rode for the sake of movement alone, not worrying about a destination, but just being present to the moment.

Nina occasionally stopped to notice something she deemed interesting—a newly sprouted leaf alone on a branch being moved by the slightest breeze, the way the sunlight fell in a dappled pattern on the forest floor of decaying leaves and pine straw, even a golfer who suddenly stopped before making her putt to notice Nina and me. The trail followed the tree line that is shared with a golf course for part of the way.

Nina and I were both more impressed by the trees than the golfer on this day. Unlike in my centering prayer practice, I don't need a word to bring me back to my intention or to focus on my breath when my mind wanders. I'm riding a horse with her own breath and intention that keeps me focused even when I'm aware of the world around me.

This world is one that lets the weight of me and my anxieties and concerns and worries fall away on the back of Nina, drip down my legs, which are dangling free of stirrups, and drop back into the deep earth to be mulched and buried until they can regrow into something useful.

In this prayer, this prayer on horseback, I am carried by Nina in our little partnership of love and companionship on a trail.

I wonder if the practices of centering prayer, meditation, and other acts of quiet solitude with God are our attempts to be carried a while by the Holy. Our souls hurt from walking in this life through the swampy, muddy ground of grief and questions and endless needs that seem overwhelming. We use so much energy explaining, and feel crushed when we aren't heard. We reach for options and alternatives that will help us find peace and quiet because we are tired.

I am tired.

And so, in prayer, I desperately want God to hold me, carry me, direct me to a mountain hideout that is a place of refuge in the midst of a world that is always in some stage of burning down. I want to find that holy, easy silence that, at least for a time, puts some space between the world and all its crazy and me. I want to be held in peace, where I can breathe and be, just simply be, without to-do lists or noise or any other static that fills my soul.

Some find that place in centering prayer or meditation or even walking along footpaths in the woods. I find this prayer of easy silence on a trail ride on Nina.

We moved together in the quiet and stillness that is the movement of horses and God. Walking, being supported, and being carried. Centering prayer and meditation, at least how I've been taught, invite practitioners, whenever we become aware of feelings, thoughts, to-do lists, or other distractions, to return to a sacred word to root ourselves in the practice. Thomas Keating wrote that this prayer practice consists in letting go of every kind of thought during prayer, even the most devout thoughts.

Maybe my prayer word is "horse," and it is not a word to be said, but a living thing to be touched and experienced.

For the time I'm on Nina, I am present in an easy silence. I hear her hooves on the path. I hear the birds move and the breeze.

My thoughts wander and fade until I am present to the slick leather of the saddle underneath me and the feel of Nina moving. I breathe in her scent deeply, that of wildness and companionship that is the smell of horses and God.

What a gift it is to find the silence that allows me to hear the breeze move, the breath of God inhale and exhale, in the world around me. When we are in the Kentucky woods together, even one that borders a golf course, the world is somewhere else, held apart for just a while as Nina carries me.

Prayer, I think, is a practice that moves us into a silence with God where we are made deeply aware of where we are, the easy silence of God and horses. This prayer, one in partnership with Nina, centers me in God.

CHAPTER 2
Drenched

❧

$\mathcal{M}$y Alabama Appalachian grandfather would have opined the rain to be a frog strangler.

My grandmother might have offered it was more of a gully washer.

I wondered if Wyoming had either frog stranglers or gully washers, pronounced more like *gully warsher* by most people in the Appalachian foothills of Alabama, except my grandmother, who had the easy, lilting accent of coastal Mississippi with so little use for *r*'s that they were dropped from the end of most words and certainly weren't added in the middle of others.

Wyoming is dry, by and large, so maybe they have little need for the colorful gradations of the rainstorms that deluge the South. The wrangler leading our trail ride simply called it a rainstorm and handed us bright yellow plastic dusters to wear as we climbed in the saddle.

Of course, in the middle of this rainstorm in the mountains of the Grand Tetons, I was on a horse. And of course, this experience of riding in a rainstorm was going to invite me to listen to God. Horses have that effect on me.

As I spread the duster's split tails over the saddle and the back of the horse, I was reminded that fashion was first and foremost functional. The duster covered my legs and most of the saddle. My inner cowgirl squealed just a bit at the image I had of myself astride a horse, wearing a duster and a cowboy hat. I stood up in the saddle to check my stirrups and quickly realized the functionality of my cowboy hat and the evidence that I didn't wear one regularly.

As I looked down to tie off a rein, a stream of rain fell straight down onto my saddle horn and into my lap from the brim of my hat. So to help the hat do its job of keeping the rain off me and onto the ground, I adapted a swagger tip to the right which had the effect of sending water onto the muddy ground, and also looking cool and cowgirl to anyone who might be watching.

This Kentucky cowgirl on a Thoroughbred/Quarter Horse cross named Maverick rode out of the paddock of standing water and mud, through a thicket of woods, and onto a trail of more mud. I shifted in the Western saddle, significantly larger than the cutback one I usually ride in. Western saddles have structure and gravitas because they are made to hold things—rope, saddlebags, rifle, rider, and even, if necessary, a calf that needs help moving from one grazing field to another (or a fellow cowboy who drank too much and can't ride his own horse home). The stirrups are likewise thick and substantial, easily allowing me to drop more of my weight into my feet as I rode.

My cutback is barely there, a sleek construction of leather made to allow the horse to move and the rider to feel almost every movement. If I ride to a bar in my cutback, only I'm riding home in it. Any friends who need a lift are on their own. Not that I regularly ride my horse to a bar, although Windy Corner, one of my favorite restaurants in Kentucky, does have a hitching post that I've seen used on occasion.

I had noticed that riding horses was not an unusual mode of transportation to watering holes in Wyoming. And I was in Wyoming, in the Bridger-Teton National Forest, riding on a muddy trail along the edge of a rise, on a horse I didn't know, sitting in a style of saddle I hadn't ridden in in well over twenty years, in a frog strangler of a rainstorm. I was dripping water and riding across old cattle trails, past a line shack with four walls, two windows, and the remains of a roof, and through vast fields of sagebrush and thistles.

I reached down to grab a handful of sagebrush as Maverick meandered by. I crushed the silver-grey leaves and petite pale-yellow flowers between my fingers and took a deep breath from the plant. The water had intensified the sage-like smell. Maverick felt me loosen the reins and angled for a thistle. We don't have wild thistle plants growing on the trails where I ride, so the epicurean delight of thistles for horses was unknown to me until Maverick informed me that thistles were, in fact, delicious. Maverick got a thistle, and I got a deep breath of rainy, sage-dense air of Wyoming.

I suspect we were both content in our drenched selves.

My first ride had been this morning, but the rain came, and the larger group of riders from the morning settled in around a fire in the great room of the ranch lodge with books, cards for a poker game, or puzzles. Four of us, including the wrangler, the woman who leads the trail ride, headed out into the Wyoming rain in early September. Our occasional yells to each other to signal low branches or that we had not fallen from our horses were the only noise that interrupted the steady harmony of rain and horse hooves sloshing along: nature's version of a candlelit church, perhaps, where something about the environs invites us not to talk except when functional.

Our voices joined the practicality of cowboy hats and dusters. Use when necessary.

Our small group of quiet, wet riders and horses came to a slope. I gave Maverick his head by dropping my hand down and forward so the reins loosened and I leaned back a bit. This allows horses to see their surroundings better to place hooves with sureness. I felt him steady his hooves and slide down the muddy embankment. Then he clopped across the wooden bridge, stopped and surveyed the path forward, which was viscous, runny mud. Maverick snorted, sounding in my mind like his derision of such an unpleasant path. He moved sideways, off the path, to create his own by crushing through the sagebrush on the side to the top of the rise. In his own time, he found the trail again. The wrangler told me he wasn't always a fan of the trail, so not to worry when he made his own, even if it seemed perilously close to the edge of a cliff or, in this case, a slide down a slope.

I did not know horses could slide in mud. I did not know the path Maverick saw, but I trusted him enough to let him take me on it. He knew the trail, the way, better than I.

Then Maverick stopped, short and suddenly. I fell forward a bit in the saddle, all the rain that had gathered on the brim of my hat unceremoniously dumping all over me. Maverick snorted and turned his head, blowing some more.

I clucked him forward. Maverick stood still. Most horses don't resist our asks for no reason, and my guess was he'd caught wind of something that he wasn't sure of, and in the Grand Tetons, it could have been any number of things, at least 73 percent of which might think Maverick and I were this evening's dinner.

And then, at the edge of the tree line, I finally saw what Maverick already knew was there—a doe and three babies. The babies continued to graze, sheltered by the canopy of trees.

The doe watched Maverick and me. Maverick and I watched them. The babies ate, ignoring all of us. The rain fell, and I paid attention.

Here I was, riding in the rain on a horse whose undiscriminating yet precise flat walk wasn't the elegant walks of my Saddlebreds, but was exactly what my wet self and the muddy trail needed. Maverick shuddered, as wet horses do, flinging the droplets from his bay coat and black mane. I breathed in the musty richness of sagebrush, the mellow scent of Maverick's wet coat, and the crisp smell of this frog strangler, gully washer rainstorm.

These were certainly the smells of heaven, right in the mountains of Wyoming.

The ends of my hair that stuck out from the cowboy hat were drenched. The lower parts of my legs not covered by the duster and my boots and my feet in my boots were drenched. My hands and the gloves that covered them were drenched.

This feeling of being drenched was also certainly a feel of heaven too.

I wondered about the generations of cowboys and cowgirls in these mountains who had ridden in the drenching rain and cursed it because they, unlike me, did not have a warm bath waiting after I put up my horse. And I wondered about those who also relished the rain, the drenching that comes with some rarity in Wyoming and maybe even in our own lives. Drenchings are needed to nourish, to wash away, to settle the dust that our often too many movements in life stir up.

The ancients of the church recognized the importance of these drenchings, these moments when rain and tears flow with gentle ferocity. Saint Benedict in his Rule observed that God regards our tears more than the many words we say in our prayers.³ Water is an important element of the stuff of faith. It's essential in the story of creation. Genesis suggests that the formless void and the water existed together as the foundational elements God used for the complexity of the vast creation. Through the waters of the Red Sea, the Hebrews passed from enslavement to freedom. We sing of this and all the mystery of water in the ancient hymn sung at the Easter Vigil, the Exsultet. Baptism, the rite of initiation into most Christian communities, involves water.

This elemental, utilitarian thing is one of the tools God uses to redeem, rescue, and restore humanity. Water is also so ubiquitous we can miss the mystical, life-giving, even destructive power of it.

In my day-to-day life, I avoid being in the rain unless I have to, which is more often than I want but certainly less often than my ancestors. Between plastic and my lifestyle, which is not as outdoorsy as past generations, I can limit my exposure to the art of a good holy drenching.

This, I think, is not good for my soul.

The part of my soul that loves horses more than the comfort of being dry had no desire to miss an opportunity to ride in the rain. After Maverick decided he'd seen enough of the deer, he turned his head toward the other riders, now a small distance in front of us. He shook again, then stepped forward, making his own path. I rode, listening to the hymn of the cushioned squish of mud as Maverick dropped his heavy hooves firmly with each step, and let the water of Wyoming, the water of creation, the water of God, drench me.

CHAPTER 3
A World of Octobers

I'm so glad I live in a world where there are Octobers,"
Anne, the title character of L. L. Montgomery's book *Anne of
Green Gables*, says, with her usual buoyant spirit of life.[4]

The story I'm about to tell wasn't from October, but the
tantalizing whisper of October moved though the breeze as I
rubbed Noah's neck on a September afternoon. He'd been a
good boy during our lesson, and now we rode on one of the
old practice racing tracks near the back of the farm.

Wingswept Farm had, in its previous life, been a training
farm for racehorses, and the oval of ground that had been
hard-packed from thousands of hooves pounding it through
the years around two ponds was still visible through the
ground cover that grew wild. The ground had earned a rest,
and now the lake area was reserved for easy rambles after
lessons to let horses and riders cool down and relax.

My legs dropped long next to Noah's sides. I rolled my
ankles as my feet relaxed in the stirrups. My hands rested on
his withers, letting the reins go lax. Noah dropped his head
slightly, his preferred angle for it.

American Saddlebreds have a natural headset that is more
upright than the lower head carriage of, say, a Quarter Horse.
Some Saddlebreds, like my Nina, like to carry their heads

higher and show off the elegant neck arch the breed is known for. Others, like Noah, would prefer not to set their heads, a phrase that means that the horse is holding her head at an arch and angle that is the hallmark of the breed.

Riding him is equivalent to arm day at the gym. He's a big boy and needs fairly constant reminders via a quick shift with the reins to keep him holding his head up and shifting his weight back, allowing him to slow gait and rack. Noah is a Saddlebred that can do five gaits—the walk, trot, and canter along with the slow gait and rack, which are essentially superenergized walks. But unlike walking, the energy for these gaits comes from the back end, which pushes a horse forward.

Noah would rather take the easy way and pull himself along with his front legs, so we work together to keep his energy and body back and me upright and balanced. And it is work.

We'd done that work on this day. I'd kept his head where it needed to be and he'd listened to my guidance, mostly. Now we rested and relaxed with a trail ride around the lake. Noah walked slowly, letting his head drop to a level angle with his body line, and I took a breath in of the air that had a chill to it. The sun was still sharing its last bit of brightness and warmth of the autumn gloss before it surrendered to the leaden shine of winter.

In Kentucky, the first scent of fall comes in mid to late September. Summer is still with us, and will be for several more weeks. But this morning, when I walked out on my back porch to let my pup, Evie, outside, the temperature had dropped enough overnight that the air had a cool and fortifying form to it, like a newly starched, gleaming white shirt back from the cleaners. I shivered a bit and felt the morning remind me that the heat and lushness of summer is not permanent. It never is.

Fall is my favorite season to ride. Horses love cooler weather. Their ideal outdoor temperature is between fifty and sixty degrees Fahrenheit. After working outside with lessons and rides in the Kentucky summer, that first taste of fall on their skin brings energy and life, just as the world outside is preparing to slumber for a while over winter. Their walks have a bit more zest and their trots are filled with a sass and vigor only autumn brings.

On this mid-September day, autumn was swirling around like a duck circling a pond trying to decide whether or not to land. And in September, autumn would not land. Not on this day. Summer would extend into a few more weeks before slowly relinquishing the deep green of leaves and grass to the reds and yellows of transition before finally giving way to pale yellows and browns.

For most of my childhood and young adulthood, I lived in a place where the transitions between seasons were, at best, brief. In the Deep South of Mississippi and Alabama, we had an extended summer with a couple of months of something that resembles winter held in place by two weeks of rain on either end. Spring does show off in the South in a particular way, but the season doesn't stay long. And autumn is fleeting.

Kentucky, however, loves autumn. Like the horses that live here, autumn is a season of vibrancy and energy, even as nature is saving hers for a long rest. Noah and I both could feel and smell the movement of the seasons today. We were motivated by the energy that gathered on our skin from the coolness that moved just slightly through the air.

Autumn is best enjoyed on the back of a horse. Noah provides an excellent vantage point, because he is a tall boy, the tallest lesson horse on the farm. His muscular, lively trot is a perfect example of what we call a lofty trot, one whose energy tosses the rider up out of the saddle so that core and leg muscles work very hard to stay balanced and focused to control the down movement back into the saddle.

Along with arm day, riding Noah is also an excellent inner thigh muscle workout. With his big, buoyant trot and kind disposition, he's a wonderful horse to ride. I smile when I ride him, laugh even, and he responds in kind with his own joy that relaxes into an after-lesson ramble to stay outside and in each other's company a bit longer. Other horses, after their lessons, have the temperament of humans on a Friday after a long week—when their lesson is over, they make haste to return to the barn for a bath, a brush, a treat, and freedom.

Noah overtly and flagrantly enjoys human relationships. His stall is the first one when we enter the lesson barn. Thus, he gets lots of nuzzles and treats, which he loves. His disposition is of a gentle curiosity. Noah is also the one horse I've fallen off of while dismounting, because I forgot how tall he was as I slid on my stomach out of the saddle. I expected both feet to land on the ground sooner than they did. I fell backward, landing on my backside. I'd let go of the reins immediately, not wanting to jerk Noah's head down with me as I fell and unsure of how he, as a young horse, would react to my falling. He shifted his head back and nuzzled my hair, checking on why his human was sitting on the ground and wondering if he could get in on the fun he was sure I was having.

A trail ride for Noah is more time in relationship before he gets dinner and rests for the evening.

On this day, Noah and I were ambling, or he was. I was sitting. His ears were pricked forward, listening to the sounds that flitter through the meadow today and to me talking to him.

I was telling him what a good big boy he was and discussing my options for dinner tonight. His ears swiveled backward to hear me. He stopped on occasion to notice something that, after a few moments, he deemed unexciting and began to walk again.

I noticed that the first of the leaves were starting to turn, and in a month, this season of red, yellow, and orange leaves, of squirrels busily gathering and burying acorns in my flowerpots, and of mornings and evenings that need a sweatshirt pulled on to keep our bodies warm will have arrived. Fall is a season of movement and of transition into winter, where my ancestors worked with focus, preparing for the winter, when the earth would lie fallow and they, to some extent, would do the same.

We modern humans don't lie fallow much anymore. Our high-tech thermal clothing and heated seats in cars allow us to carry on with our lives regardless of the amount of snow and cold outside. Our food, once guided mostly by the seasons, now simply shifts from hemisphere to hemisphere, so we eat strawberries and tomatoes all year round, or at least something that resembles them after being shipped from across the globe.

Yet fall is a particular time for me to remember the Sabbath: Sabbath as a day of rest, and our created world with Sabbath seasons as well. Spring and summer are seasons of action in the human world and in the horse world. We are preparing for the immediacy of show season, working during lessons to lift our riding a notch. The horses are in shape and ready to be their best. Then fall slides in, and we see the end of shows on the calendar. The spring and summer riding routine begins to shift and change as we enter into fall and ready for winter.

The number of riders diminishes as the temperatures drop. Winter is the season of the die-hard regulars who ride. I still ride in the winter. My barn has an indoor heated arena, but indoor riding is a bit different: no after workout trail rides, for one thing.

In our agrarian world, we were more aware of the shifts and changes and how they shifted and changed us. The holy places where things shift and change intrigue me, especially the ones that invite us to rest, to return to fallowness.

Sabbath does that. A time of rest reminds me that my work will remain undone and incomplete. I am moved from production to presence. Sabbath can be a particular religious observance, a season, or even a ride on Noah after a lesson.

Did we accomplish something in our lesson today?

Yes.

Is our work together done?

No.

Noah still has things to teach me as a rider, and I have things to teach him as a horse. I am acutely aware that when I first began riding him, I was a bit scared of his canter. Like most five-gaited horses, his canter is big, made even bigger by his size. My first few rides on him were frustrating because I was fearful of riding his canter.

Until I realized I wasn't anymore. I was present to his canter and to my own riding, and our resting time on the trail rides gave me time to trust him, to talk with him, to know him. And the feeling is likely mutual. Now, I really enjoy cantering Noah, although Alyssa, one of the instructors at Wingswept, notes that I enjoy letting him gallop a bit more than canter. Being present to a trusting relationship with a horse does that.

As I rode Noah through a meadow giving up the last breath of summer, I was acutely aware of the wisdom of the change of seasons and the movement to an extended time of rest and quietness and wonder how much better off humans would be if we listened to them.

October is coming soon. The days are here when I wear long sleeves and a jacket in the morning, but by afternoon I have shed my clothing to something cooler. Then the coolness returns with the sunset and it has me reaching for more clothing once again.

Horses begin to grow thicker fur, and almost overnight the sleekness of summer is replaced by the teddy bear fluff that will keep them warmer. We can no longer easily hose them off after a ride, but instead rub them down with towels until they are dry and let them stand with a cooler to keep them warm until we blanket them.

Nina loves Octobers because she loves blankets. I remind myself to check and make sure she will be warm enough as the first fall cold arrives tonight. Nina has a lovely ability to help you put all her blankets on her so she can be warm and cozy on chilly nights.

She knows how to change with the season, how to be present to a time of rest and quietness. Noah does as well.

I wonder if I do.

Fall for me, for many of us, is the beginning of the school year, the program year, and the endless holiday season that seems to almost start in August these days. In Kentucky, where I live, the days become shorter and colder. The natural world begins to settle down for rest, an extended Sabbath time to curl up in burrows under our own blankets with our stash of food and a good book, doing what is necessary but not much more.

Maybe this September and October, as we move into winter, I can be like Noah on the trail—a bit more aware of the new things that appear, letting my soul adapt as things change. His ears are very busy, noticing all manner of sounds, from the construction workers yelling at each other while replacing the roof on the house in the neighborhood across the street, to the chipmunks maniacally zipping from one side of the trail to the other on their daily business of readying for winter. My skin is very aware too. I feel the change. My human skin, with all its receptors and ways to communicate, is telling me to pay attention.

Noah and my Sabbath trail ride linger in my soul as I recall the "Prayer for Quiet Confidence" from the Book of Common Prayer:

> O God of peace, who hast taught us that in returning and rest we shall be saved, in quietness and in confidence shall be our strength. By the might of thy Spirit lift us, we pray thee, to thy presence, where we may be still and know that thou art God; through Jesus Christ our Lord. Amen.[5]

Returning and rest, quietness and stillness, are as important as active accomplishment. Autumn is coming, and winter is slipping into the starting gate, waiting for its turn. Creation in Kentucky will settle and wait. Horses rest. Humans could rest, too, if we remember the value of a season of rest and quietness.

"I'm so glad I live in a world where there are Octobers," Anne says in *Anne of Green Gables.* Yes, I'm so thankful we have a world and a faith where the changes remind me to return and rest, and this time of rest is hallowed.

CHAPTER 4
Wide-Open

———— ❧ ————

$\mathcal{T}$he entire state of Wyoming is open—wide-open. Yes, there are towns with buildings settled together along streets with people, yet even there, a wide-openness pervades. I noticed on my stroll through Dubois, about an hour from Jackson, that people noticed you, nodded, even tipped their cowboy hats and baseball caps, and said hello, all with a graciousness that acknowledged me and that served as a reminder that space mattered. You stay in your space, and I'll stay in mine.

Wyoming is a state that embodies the adjective *wide-open*. Spread your arms and scream loudly and the odds are, only the coyotes and elk will hear you, so keep screaming. The population of the entire state is only about 200,000 more than the city of Lexington, Kentucky, where I live. Yet it's over 97,500 square miles larger.

Most of us live in considerably more confined spaces. When I lived in New York, I could hear one neighbor flush his toilet through our shared hallway wall and smell another neighbor's cooking escapades across the air shaft. Even in Lexington, the space is restrained around me. When I crack my windows on the north side of my home in the fall, I enjoy listening to my neighbors' graceful mumblings as they sit around their firepit.

Security is a fine need for us humans, the soft blanket of safety that is swaddled around our souls when we feel too vulnerable, too exposed, and too unsettled by the things that go bump in our dark nights. Faith offers that security in the liturgies of our practices—when we bow our head at the name of Jesus or cross ourselves at the end of a prayer, the prayers we've said so many times they exist in our bones more than our intellect, so that when we are shaken to our core and we respond by instinct, the instinctual prayers come.

Our Father, who art in heaven.

Hail Mary, full of grace.

Lord Jesus Christ, son of God, have mercy on me, a sinner.

Faith offers that option, to curl up in the corner with God and wrap myself in a familiarity of prayers that comfort me in my cubbyhole. I am secure. I am safe. I am stacked against others in this faith and in this life. I am not alone.

And yet, my faith also needs time alone, when I wander in the desert or in the back country of Bridger-Teton National Forest on a horse. I need solitude, periods of unescorted meandering through life, often in conditions that are uncomfortable, muddy, and even risky. Jesus needed time alone. The Gospels of Matthew, Mark, Luke, and John regularly have accounts of Jesus going away to quiet places.

A life of faith is lived in both the security of certainty and familiarity and the adventure of being out there alone with God, stretching out our arms in the middle of nowhere, throwing our head back to catch the rain, yelling for only the audience of God and ourselves, and knowing we are so far out in the vastness that safety and security are a few miles back at the last watering hole or the old line shack with a roof mostly intact.

I passed that line shack on Maverick, and now we had taken a series of trails that led to the very edge of one of the mountaintops. To get here, our small band of riders and horses took a route that may have been a horse trail or one regularly used by animals to reach the peak. Maverick didn't seem to care, as long as I let him wander off the trail when the rocks bothered him. As we rode, the early morning clouds burned away to an afternoon of glorious sun. The mountain air of Wyoming lets colors be shaded differently from the colors of Lexington. The air in Wyoming creates a gloss that intensifies colors, at least up this high. The blue sky was searingly blue. The browns and greens of the grasslands were raw, rich pigments deeply settled in the grass, dirt, and trees. I could even see the full gradations of red and brown with flecks of black hairs in Maverick's bay coat in this sunlight and atmosphere.

I pushed my reins forward so Maverick could freely pump his head to have the momentum to go up this trail that was looking less like a horse trail as we went, but we were almost to the top. I leaned forward in the saddle, even standing out of the saddle a bit so Maverick could maneuver the steep, narrow climb. I looked up and forward to see the line where earth and sky meet and the Teton mountains stitch them together with their sharp peaks.

From this vantage point, a new one, things looked different. Once we topped the trail that maybe was a horse trail but it got us to the top, we came to a plateau and could see clearly the condescending glory that is the Grand Teton range—not from below, but from across. The beauty of it all is almost too much, as if my senses could only take in small parts because the whole of it is overpowering.

The Tetons rise up out of a flat plain area, an unusual geographical feature. The fires burning in California had encased the range in a smoky haze for the past few days, but the rain yesterday cleared the miasma and left clarity. I dropped my stirrups and let my legs rest on Maverick's side. We both looked across the valley at the Tetons. Maverick's ears framed the vastness of Wyoming. They provided a furry frame for this view of God.

The bigness of creation reminds me of the smallness of me. And yet, being on Maverick, my companion on this spiritual journey through the Tetons with occasional breaks for him to snack on a thistle, my soul remembered how to be present in the vastness of God without being lost in the minuteness of being human.

God is out there, in the unknown, the unfamiliar, and the places that saturate us in something new. Our experiences of God are also found in the wide-open vastness, where the expectations and presumptions of other people can fall away, and we find ourselves with God, perhaps able finally to hear the still, small voice that can only be heard in the midst of nothingness and an occasional elk bugle.

These moments of wide-open vastness are harder and harder to experience in our city life, in our busy lives of constant connection and text messages, in the presence of others who bump into us and don't even acknowledge us. Perhaps that is why so many people hike, camp, and find the wide-open spaces where they can, when they can. That is certainly why I was in the vastness of Wyoming on a horse.

Not that I came out here for that specific reason: no, I just wanted to ride horses in the Mountain West. That was my thinking. My soul, however, had a more subversive motivation. My soul needed to be wide open with God. She was weary of homesteading in the familiar and the crowded spaces. My soul had homesteaded long enough, and needed to find some new trails to explore. I needed to move away from the familiar into the places that dared me to shrink back, but also dared me to trust an unknown horse on a sketchy trail up to somewhere vast.

I am by nature a homesteader. I find the home base, the ground under my feet that has been trod by eons of ancestors, that has absorbed the prayers of joy and the laments of grief, and that has gotten underneath my fingernails.

But I am not only a homesteader, and God dares me to strike out, even if for a month. Jesus doesn't homestead. He moved. He moves. We move. We step into our first experience of us in a new place, and God opens a newness to us, about us.

As a longtime horse rider, I find simply being with horses restores my soul. Horses are where I always find the presence of God. As a priest, I find God when I celebrate the Eucharist. As a person of faith, I meet God in prayer. And I'm also aware I'm often the one worrying about the prayers and the Mass. Are the candles all lit? Are the chalice and paten set on the altar, ready for the celebration? Is that Ms. Richardson's daughter with her today? She told me she'd ended her marriage. I need to remember to check in with her after the service.

This is the narrative that shares space with the yearning to be present fully with God as I preside at Mass or at any service of prayer. It's quite a privilege, and it exhausts my soul one small detail at a time. I feel, often, as anyone who has responsibilities and demands—and my guess is that's all of us—that all these responsibilities and demands close in on our souls like one brick being built around us at a time, stifling our soul's vitality and energy. Our movements become limited. Our muscles move one way. And our view becomes blocked.

My soul felt stuck in the closed, small space of worry. Life will do that to me, to us. While these small spaces are useful, they can't be our only spaces. We can't move, we can't stretch, we can't see, and we can't wander—all things necessary for flourishing.

So, I did what every woman who loves horses and God and needs to stretch again does—I ran off to the Mountain West to a ranch in Wyoming, near the Grand Tetons. I looked at the openness, the vastness that I'd not seen because all the other details of a busy life demanded my attention. Or, if I was more honest, I'd let the details of life take my attention.

But not here: right here, touching the forest line, was openness, the physical space of the prayer life I need—we all need. Here was the place to stretch and move and heal, even. Small and strongly secure has its place in our faith, but so does openness and movement. When I broke my ribs (via a horse fall, of course), I expected to have them wrapped and steadied to heal.

"No," the doctor said, "Some bones heal better when they are allowed to move."

Moving broken ribs is not comfortable, and we use our ribs with literally every breath and laugh and sneeze.

Oh, do we use them when we sneeze.

But ribs are protective bone made to move, so they do, indeed, heal better when they are not bound, but allowed to move with our breath.

Souls live better when they are allowed to move. Mine is one. Life can too often feel walled up and small, contrasting to a Jesus who is all about the wide-open spaces of love and courage and life. Jesus and Maverick asked me to look up and out into the vastness of creation in this holy church of Wyoming, to notice, to breathe and feel too big and too tiny all at once, because on this plateau ridiculously upward and standing across from the Grand Tetons, I was.

CHAPTER 5
Mule Motivation

*T*he wrangler handed me what she called a "mule motivator," a woven leather handle with several pieces of leather hanging from it. I'd seen something that looked similar in the Tower of London's display of tools used for torture. Mules, however, are not tortured by a swift tap from the mule motivator.

They are motivated.

People who aren't familiar with horses are often troubled that many riders use a crop or a whip or spurs as we ride. "It hurts the horses!" they often say.

Like many training tools humans use with animals, yes, they can cause hurt when wielded inappropriately and in anger. But more often, even most often, they are ways we communicate with horses. In the wild and in the paddock, horses nip and kick each other to communicate.

My using a crop, even firmly, is considerably less intense than a fiery kick from a horse who has had enough of whatever behavior another horse is doing to annoy them. A gentle tap on their shoulder gets a horse's attention when something else is distracting them. A firmer tap may remind the horse that I am indeed riding and I expect good manners from my horses. And, on occasion, a reach around tap on their hind end, the riding equivalent of "you made me stop the car and come back there," corrects some significantly unhelpful behavior.

I'd never ridden a mule before the day I stood in the middle of a paddock with a line of both people and saddled mules. I was at the end of the line with my friends. I swished the mule motivator around, getting used to its feel in my hand. The head wrangler moved down the line, asking each person about their riding experience and assigning them to a commensurate mule. Our group was made up of many people who had never ridden.

When he got to me, he looked at his list. "Please tell me you've ridden before."

"I've been on a horse a few times," I replied, hoping my answer wouldn't lead to me riding an ill-tempered mule on the edge of the Grand Canyon. My friend Brad laughed. "Yeah, just a few," he said.

A few minutes later, I was sitting in a Western saddle on my transport for the day, a mule named Gracie. Gracie was a fan of doing her own thing, the head wrangler said, as I checked the length of my stirrups and got used to the feel of the single rein in my hands.

"Aren't we all," I replied, scratching Gracie's neck.

The wrangler and the trail guides instructed us all to walk our mules around the ring. They rambled off the basics of riding—how to get your mule to stop or walk, how to keep them spaced, and how not to fall off.

This last point was very pointedly directed as a reminder that when you are riding a mule, your first priority is not trying to get the perfect photograph of the Grand Canyon while letting your reins drop. That, the wrangler suggested, is a good way to lose your balance when the mule realizes no one is in control and decides to dash off at a good clip back to the corral. After the talks about how to ride, we were off, our merry band of twelve riders to ride the South Rim of the Grand Canyon.

Mules have a long history with the Grand Canyon. Mules are the offspring of a jack (male donkey) and a mare (female horse). Mules have the head features of the donkey and the body features of the horse. They are the size of their dam, but have the temperament of a donkey, which is to say, they are less skittish and have greater endurance than horses, but are faster and more agile than donkeys. Although few scientific studies exist, many trainers will say a horse has the intelligence of a human three-year-old and a mule, of a human four-year-old. They also eat less than horses of similar size, which makes them perfect for explorers and farmers.

Mules are spectacularly sure-footed. Their hybrid eyes are located just a bit further apart than horses' eyes, so mules can see all four feet and place their hind hooves in the exact places where their front hooves just were. They also have smaller hooves that are more vertical than horse hooves; that is, their hooves aren't as wide but are taller. Smaller hooves help when maneuvering through rocky and uneven terrain, which the Grand Canyon most definitely is.

When mules spook, they generally stop and stand. Horses, from experience, spook with far greater drama. Standing still is almost never an option for some horses when jumping sideways, spinning, or rearing is such a better response to the plastic bag blowing across the field, the miniature donkey in the next paddock, or a leaf.

This quality alone makes it easy to see why mules became the mammal of choice for going up and down steep mountain paths and rocky canyon trails.

And mules have wonderful ears. Their ears are bigger than horse ears. Equine ears are as expressive as a Southern woman's eyebrows. Equine ears are a tool of communication for them and a way humans can understand them. Ear position tells me if a horse is attentive, bored, or angry. The larger size of mule ears is a function of dissipating heat, since donkeys seem to have evolved in a desert environment and larger ears gave more surface area to allow body heat to release.

I, of course, was reveling in all things mule as I rode Gracie. Her ears were rotating attentively backward, listening to me tell her how fluffy she was. I'm a sucker for a fluffy horse—or mule. I ran my hands over her withers, noting how much wider they were than those of the horses I rode. I felt her gait under me rock with a particular smoothness, even as she carefully stepped her way over some fallen branches.

"Are you even looking?" Brad asked me, reminding me that we were, indeed, riding around the South Rim of the Grand Canyon.

Oh, right. That.

I was looking, except I was looking at the mule. The newness of this particular equine was absolutely intriguing to me. Since I was riding drag (the back position in a line of mules or horses), I held Gracie back a bit to let her trot. I wanted to feel how she moved at the trot. Gracie was not as lofty as my Saddlebreds, but she had a sweet rock to her trot that would have made riding long distances across the vastness of the West quite comfortable.

Our mule train stopped to look over a part of the Grand Canyon not accessible to tourists except to those on mule. There were Native American ruins underneath us, in the edge of the canyon. From certain angles I could see squared-off edges that may have been constructed buildings or just the way the wind and weather shaped the stone.

I leaned forward to rub Gracie's ears some more and took a deep breath. The late winter smells of pine and mule gave depth to the astonishment that was the Grand Canyon.

We'd hiked from the rim to near the floor two days before. It was not an easy trip. Partway down, we had to scurry up the side of some rocks to let a mule train pass. In that moment, time folded inside itself and I watched the sure-footed, sturdy creatures walk nose to tail with supplies strapped to their backs. Some places in our world don't care that we have cars or even helicopters to move people or things, so we use the things we have used for eons. We walk. We boat. Or we use mules or horses.

The old ways aren't always obsolete and can, in fact, motivate us forward in our journey.

New and shiny is seductive and alluring. I regularly read essays and e-mails and watch short videos touting the new prayer practice or book or program that will deepen my faith, strengthen my relationship with God, and grow the church.

Faith has been commoditized like a newer model car. Sure, the faith you have is good, but does it have this new software design that interfaces with your watch and phone to remind you to read a short reflection on today's passage from the Bible or tell you when there's a traffic jam and reroute you?

Don't get me wrong. Newness is good and holy. I need to see my faith from different points of view and try new things. God is changeless and changing, always opening us to new ways to love ourselves and each other while building on the classic commandment to love. And yet, when I get overwhelmed with all that is life and I've reached for so much newness to reinvigorate my faith that I find myself holding on to nothing, the emptiness often motivates me to go back to the beginning.

I did not grow up on horseback; I did grow up in the church. Two of my great-grandfathers were pastors. My seventh great-grandfather was an Anglican priest who left England and pastored First Church in Salem several decades before the tragic murder of so many women there by fellow congregants. Another great-grandfather helped found the Disciples of Christ. My family is filled with Sunday school teachers and itinerant preachers. The denominations have been varied, but my roots in the flavors of the Christian church run deep and sprawling.

Perhaps those sprawling roots mean I come legitimately by my curious nature, the what's new, what's different, what's around the corner that I need to see and explore. Those motivate me. They intrigue me, discovering these new things for my faith, my ministry, my life.

Like mule motivators and crops, they are helpful. And, used too much, they are hurtful.

So my unhelpful response is to throw all these tools to the ground. I don't need any of them. Also, I'm tired. I sit, mad about all of it. I find myself stopped on the path. Not moving. Stuck.

God has mule motivators, too, for the four-year-olds in our souls that need to be reminded to sit as long as we need to sit, but then get up and go when that time comes. God motivates me to meander back around to the old ways, the things that brought me into the church in the first place. Not the church I inherited, but the church I discovered for myself. I walked into the Episcopal Church not because I'd done research on theology or explored position statements, but because a friend invited me and I went.

And there, in the midst of a slate stone floor and wooden beams that crossed overhead to hold up the roof, between the altar and the back pew, where I sat, I experienced God for myself—not in the youth revival emotion of my youth or the clap-back intellectualism of my college days, but the words of the Mass.

Take. Eat. This is my Body.

Drink this, all of you. This is my Blood of the new covenant.

Sanctify us, that we may serve you.

And I heard these words prayed while I knelt. Now, for those who grew up in certain denominations, kneeling as a prayer posture was likely not the new thing it was for me that Sunday.

I discovered this new thing that Sunday, this physical engagement of my self and soul that let me fold down into a small space where I could be with God and not be distracted by the world around me. Kneeling in that space, I felt protected as I communed with God. The sounds of others shifting and kneeling in prayer, of the priest placing wafers on the paten and the movements of the altar servers getting ready to share the Body and Blood with us, all created an environment of ordinary holiness.

The words of the Eucharist, kneeling in silence, receiving the host, gathered in community with people who come from their lives to this place, together, motivated my soul to recognize the need I had for God, for mystery, and for a faith community—not that I processed all that exactly in that way after my first Sunday. But my soul reached out for the Body of Christ in the host and held it in my hands. I was in a vulnerable place, and I felt safe.

I went back. And went back. And kept going back. I discovered saints and holy days of obligation and novenas—all the new stuff. I reveled in it, let it fill me until I overflowed with joy and eagerness and overwhelmed myself with all things nifty and new about this incarnation of faith in the Episcopal Church. Until I needed to go back to what drew me in in the first place, the God that met me as I knelt. The God who found me in smallness and quietness.

The old things return me to myself, to the reasons my soul leapt at the presence of God in the beginning. The miracle of God is that I don't return to the old things as my old self. I bring all the newness, all the insights my ventures and explorations have taught me and exposed me to. And there, in the old ways of kneeling in silence, of saying the prayers whose words I've repeated hundreds and even perhaps thousands of times, I rediscover me.

Gracie was a new creature, but she reminded me of the old practices I'd learned from riding—how to sit up and sit deep in the saddle; how to hold the reins with enough pressure so she knows I'm there and directing her, but not so much that I'm annoying her; and how to motivate her to go where I'd like her to go. All those old things, those old ways, gave me the tools to explore this new treasure of riding a mule in the Grand Canyon.

I looked at the majesty of God's creation, made by time and wind and rain and rock, through Gracie's ears, and said the oldest prayer I knew.

Thank you.

CHAPTER 6
In Forward

My great-aunt died well before I was born, but at our annual Moore family reunions, my surviving great-aunts and their children would weave the memories of those relatives who had died in years past into the fabric of our present. Anytime one of the latest generations got their driver's licenses, we would hear the story of Aunt Tote and her ingenious driving ability or, actually, complete lack of it.

Aunt Tote could only drive her car in forward.

Zella Jane, my Aunt Tote's given name that was unknown to me until I was well into my adulthood when I dabbled in genealogy and visited her grave, was one of the eight surviving children of my great-great-grandparents, TJ and Belle Moore. TJ and Belle settled near the Standing Pine Choctaw Reservation in Mississippi, where my great-great-grandfather learned Latin and Greek by correspondence courses as he farmed their plot of land and taught at the Standing Pine school. At almost forty, which in the late nineteenth century was a ripe old age, he was ordained a Baptist minister. He sold his farm and became pastor of Carthage Baptist Church.

Belle and TJ's life and ministry was in rural Mississippi, ranging from Choctaw Reservation communities to rough- and-tumble mill towns. In the midst of moves, with barely enough money to put food on the table, and a commitment to a life of discipleship, they made sure their children were faithful and dutiful Christians, and all graduated from college, quite amazing in the early twentieth century for a Baptist minister with seven daughters.

When one of us would ask about Aunt Tote or Aunt Emma or one of the other eight children, the descriptions almost always began with, "She was a faithful Christian."

That's not a particularly unusual descriptor of people in the Deep South. My people say "faithful Christian" or its synonym "good Christian person" when describing someone as often as we say, "Bless their heart," when hearing about regretful or tragic news involving someone. The real skill is translating the true meaning of those phrases.

Sometimes they are simply words to fill the space in a conversation. Sometimes they mean the exact opposite. Southerners, or at least many of the ones I grew up around, would rather step on their own lips with golf shoes than utter a mean word against someone in public. So "Bless your heart" is often code for "No one is surprised those Jacobs boys singed all their hair off with fireworks at the church revival. None of that family has the sense God gave a goose."

And let's not even talk about what "She was a faithful Christian" might mean. But at least for my great-aunts and one great-uncle, that duplicitous declaration was followed up with context.

These daughters and one son of a couple who preached the gospel in Mississippi volunteered in hospitals and in the military (yes, even the women). They started schools in rural communities and opened their homes to those who needed shelter from the weather and from life, without question.

The span of generations has likely edited out the snarls and edges of the narratives in between the high points, so that the canon of their lives has been veiled with kindness. But there are moments of our lives, even in the lives of saints and great-aunts, that demand attention because they are simply so . . . other, so peculiar that they invite us to smile and nod at the beautiful, weird humanity of the person.

Which is why I love that Aunt Tote could only drive in forward. She never married, which, in the decades when she lived her adult life, was either scandalous or tragic, depending on which group of women gathered in the parking lot after church to discuss her.

She had a career, working all her adult life for Southern Bell Telephone and Telegraph as operator and eventually chief operator. She paid the college tuition of her nieces and nephews. She got them jobs at the phone company, and she gave them adventure as only a woman named Zella could do.

Yes, Aunt Tote was an adventurer, albeit only in forward.

She drove across the country and explored all manner of small towns and whistle-stops in the era of routes and highways that meandered through towns. She took her nieces with her, including my grandmother. And she did it in forward.

Aunt Tote could drive—just not in reverse.

I've never discerned in family lore how exactly she managed this particular skill, or lack of it. I'm assuming cars in the twenties and thirties were more challenging to drive than my Subaru today, which lets me know if I'm too close to the car in front of me or not staying in my lane and will text me if my tire pressure is low.

She decided my grandmother and my three grand aunts needed to see the West. Young women needed to see wildness, which in her Southern soul, meant the world beyond the Mississippi River. She gathered them and set out from Baton Rouge, Louisiana, in her Model A Ford to see the West—San Antonio, El Paso, Carlsbad Caverns, and the Grand Canyon among the highlights. They stayed with Tote's friends from her years in the phone industry and in rustic cottages, which my grandmother used to say were charming and agreeable until I asked her in her later years about them, and she opined that they were a step above the abandoned house down the road that had a peach tree growing through the floorboards in the front room and was also haunted, according to neighbors.

They ate peanut butter and jelly at roadside stops and each night, everyone took a dose of Milk of Magnesia.

My grandmother remembered that trip, her first real adventure beyond visiting relatives and friends in Mississippi towns. She said the trip was her first real glimpse of the vastness of God. After all, Mississippi didn't have deserts or grand canyons. Even the Milk of Magnesia was a fondly held memory.

"And at every place we stayed, Aunt Tote would have one of us get out and make sure she parked in a place she could get out of, because she could only drive in forward, you know."

Being able to reverse is a helpful skill in driving, but I think Aunt Tote's unabashed movement forward is something to be admired, especially in her life that spanned fifty-nine years when she died in 1946. She moved forward into her life, her adventure, with peanut butter and jelly and Milk of Magnesia.

She traveled with herself, alone. Somewhere in family lore is that she was courting a young pilot who died in World War One, and she decided she'd never meet someone as agreeable for her as he was, so she decided to marry herself. That's living in forward in an era that defined women mostly by their marriage status and the children they had.

In the midst of California, the state in which Aunt Tote drove forward until she could loop around to return home by her path forward again, I stood in the courtyard of the Carmel Mission, the church and mission founded by Junipero Serra. He was a Franciscan and an academic until, after twenty years of that life, he went forward into the New World (the part that eventually became California) and established a series of missions. He argued with the political elite and brought Christianity to thousands of indigenous peoples living in the area. Both of those events brought harm and good and deep wounds and a complex legacy.

The Mission has his motto engraved on various stones and walls—"Always keep moving forward."

As I looked at the quote, I wondered, "Who always keeps moving forward?"

Don't we need to go backward, to revisit the past and our choices and mistakes. Isn't that what we call contemplation?

The still-annoying question rolled through my mind as I rode horses with a friend later that day at a local ranch. She'd never ridden and was making the mistake almost all new riders do and quite a few of us who've ridden for years or decades still do on occasion—pulling back on the reins without releasing.

Pulling back on the reins when done in a short movement, followed by a release and often the word, "Whoa," tells the horse to stop. Pulling back constantly, without stopping, tells the horse to back up. But even then, I release the reins once the horse is moving in the backward direction. Horses aren't really made to back up in long distances. They can back up for short distances, to move out of the way, maneuver toward the feed bucket, or back into the tacking area so we can put on saddles and bridles. But their hind end is in one of their blind spots, so eventually, most horses will become fearful and even panicked if we keep pulling backward, and they may eventually rear up, flip over, or fall. Neither is an ideal option for a rider or a horse.

"Hands forward," I said to her. "Remember to keep your hands forward and let your horse go forward."

"Do we ever want them to back up?" my friend asked.

"Sometimes, but not constantly. Better to turn around, then go forward and retrace your path than go backward and risk disaster."

Humans like to go forward; we like always to keep moving forward. Most of us get agitated when our forward progress is stifled: when we're hurrying to get through the grocery store and someone is slowly meandering down the aisle that we need to zip through to get to our next stop; when we are going nowhere fast in stop-and-go traffic; when we go to renew our car tag and see the line is at least seventeen miles long.

At least in our US culture, we are wired always to keep moving forward.

Which is slightly different from what my Aunt Tote modeled, for reasons known only to her. Yes, she could only drive forward, but stories of the vacation with the nieces and other aspects of her life have many moments of slowing down, even stopping. She could only drive forward, but she stopped to see the Grand Canyon, to eat at mom and pop diners, and to stay with friends. I can imagine, with some justification from family traits, that she talked to people as she stopped. She asked about the recipe for the apple pie or wondered where the closest drug store was so she could buy some more Milk of Magnesia.

Always going forward may feel like constant accomplishment, but the moments where we stop, where we are sometimes forced to move more slowly, allow us to catch our breath and notice. Slow and even stop gives us the pace to reflect on our past and contemplate our present and discern our future.

The lesson I've learned from horses is that we often forget we have a blind spot with what's behind us, and constantly wanting to move backward isn't the safest option. Constantly revisiting choices and mistakes, mulling over regret, and even living in the halcyon memories of the past that are usually hazy with nostalgia rather than clear with reality leave us stuck. Horses would rather turn and face what's behind them or revisit what they missed the first time around than back up blindly and risk significant harm to themselves and those around them.

Different times demand different approaches to movement. For a Franciscan priest with a vast land he wanted to settle with missions, perhaps always moving forward was the spiritual speed that seemed plausible for him. For my Aunt Tote, moving forward at various paces was her only option because reverse, at least in a car, was something she either couldn't master or, more likely, decided not to master. But for me, I've found that the temptation to move forward at a constant speed is exhausting to my soul. I, like horses, can't gallop constantly.

I can, however, spend a voluminous amount of time going backward blindly. Doing so is a favorite hobby of mine, as a recovering perfectionist. Perfectionism is the sin of thinking I, somehow, am above making mistakes, and when I do, I must revisit and reflect and move backward until I figure out what, exactly, went wrong.

The reality of this is that while I imagine myself being contemplative about all this reflection, I am really just backing up blindly.

Riding has taught me the value of moving backward just enough, then turning and facing what needs to be explored. Someone needs to pull the reins just enough, then know when to stop and let us turn around. The value of a guide and helper when we do have to go backward is that they help pull us just far enough, then let us stop and rest. Guides may even know when we need to be turned around so we can see better.

Just the way I watched Nina do in the field one day when she was turned out with another horse. A flock of geese were grazing in a nearby field when the neighbor's dog decided to bound into the middle of their lunch. The ensuing kerfuffle was behind Nina, so she turned her whole body to look. All thousand pounds of her faced the questionable noise. She pricked her ears forward and shifted her head, standing so still she wasn't even chewing the grass blades that dangled from her mouth. After a few moments, she discerned that whatever was going on was far enough from her so she was in no danger. Then she turned back around, lowered her head, and resumed her grazing.

Self-reflectiveness is a holy gift that can quickly find us stuck, moving blindly backward. I relive old family dramas, past job decisions, and even the way I ended Sunday's sermon. How could I have made a different decision? Did Jane hear that sermon the wrong way? What if I'd never taken that job?

I can back myself up and flip myself over with the what ifs and whys. It's an exhausting expression of self-doubt masquerading as contemplation. Maybe I need to remember the lessons from Aunt Tote and Nina.

Move forward.

Stop to look back when something needs attention. If it does, turn and face it, getting a good sense of what it is.

If it doesn't need my attention, go back to the trail, and keep moving.

PART TWO
IN THE ARENA

It is not the critic who counts. . . . The credit belongs to the man who is actually in the arena, whose face is marred by dust and sweat and blood; who strives valiantly; who errs, who comes short again and again, because there is no effort without error and shortcoming; but who does actually strive to do the deeds; who knows great enthusiasms, the great devotions; who spends himself in a worthy cause; who at the best knows in the end the triumph of high achievement, and who at the worst, if he fails, at least fails while daring greatly, so that his place shall never be with those cold and timid souls who neither know victory nor defeat.

—THEODORE ROOSEVELT, from his speech *Citizenship in a Republic* given at the Sorbonne, Paris, April 23, 1910

Just ride the damn horse.

—STEPHANIE BRANNAN (my instructor)

*F*or me, the arena is a holy space, a building (or fence) that provides the container for learning, for prayer, for instruction, some rejoicing, and more than a few sermons from both horses and my instructors on how to put the words of riding into practice.

I can read any number of books on riding (and I have), watch videos on how to sit a rocking canter, and listen to experts talk about horsemanship, but until I actually get on a horse and in the arena, I'm engaging in a purely intellectual exercise.

Not that the intellectual part of riding or faith is useless. It's certainly not.

The Epistle to James tells us faith without works is dead. Jesus consistently reminds us in his teachings that words matter, as well as actions. I can't be a person of faith without a relationship with God and, by extension, other humans. And I can't be an equestrian without a relationship with horses and the riding that forms that relationship.

The arena is the holy place for this work, this often hard work, of relationship. Riding a horse is not a matter of unidirectional commands. Riding is a relationship between a rider and a horse, both who have ideas, personalities, quirks, and shortcomings. Riding is a partnership of independent thinkers with their own mindsets, which can be frustrating, but it is also filled with life and distinction. When I ride, I realize what I don't know and learn that what I do know has its limits, especially when I'm riding a horse who is testing those limits.

I was feeling that today on Fatimo.

"So this is the way it's going to be," I sighed, shifting a bit in the saddle and rolling my knees in as I dropped even more of my backside into the saddle to encourage Fatimo that a flat walk would be a good idea.

His continued jogging prance slowed a bit. I exhaled again and rolled back on my pockets just a bit more to sit even deeper until, finally, he conceded to the flat walk.

Fatimo is a baby. Not really, but he was a four-year-old when many of us first rode him. He was and still is a bit skittish and jumpy about life, and his baby-ness has been our shorthand for his particular personality. He's a bit nervous about fences, doorways, and riding crops, to name a few things. He's also a skinny boy, which means the lovely chub of some horses that makes holding on with my thighs and knees easier is not available on him.

"He's got lots of baby energy," we'd say when he jumped at the sight of an open door: the same open door that he'd trotted by dozens of times before, but this time it was scary. He's not a baby anymore. He is young, and he is still energetic and excitable.

Less so, though. Sometimes he's calmer, and my rides on him are easier than they were.

Not, however, today. Lately Fatimo has decided he's unhappy when riders hold a crop, a straight whip, essentially, used to get a horse's attention. Riders do not use crops to beat a horse. We use a crop to get the horse to notice us. We tap a horse, even hold it out so they can see it to divert their attention if they want to shy away from a corner or whatever seems scary to them.

For reasons known only to Fatimo, he has decided a crop is one riding aid too much for him.

For a horse used to teach people how to ride, that is not helpful. Horses used in riding lessons need to be mostly okay with crops so that riders can learn to use them appropriately. So today, I suggested I would drop the crop because Fatimo was still unsettled. A father watching his child ride took off his baseball cap to wipe the sweat off his forehead at the very moment we were trotting by, sending him in a sideways jump that reminded me why we hold on and balance with thighs and not hands.

My instructor said no. Clearly.

"Ride him with the crop. Make him halt, reverse, and walk. With manners."

Our first attempt at a halt and reverse to change directions did not result in a walk. Fatimo decided a gallop would be acceptable. I gently wiggled his bit and sat deeply in the saddle to get his attention and talked to him in the horse language that says, "We could stop galloping now and walk."

Fatimo finally agreed after two laps around the arena. He sort of walked, prancing and huffing a bit, probably a blend of his sudden expelling of energy in the gallop and his opinion of my request to walk when he wasn't sure he wanted to walk.

I offered a singsong of "Whoa walk," as we moved around the arena, a lullaby to a not really baby horse who was doing the best he could and needed a reminder of just what that best could look like.

"I'm not dropping the crop, so this is the way it's going to be," I shared with Fatimo.

I shared this with myself too. I wanted to drop the crop. I thought it would calm him down and make for an easier ride for me. It might, but Fatimo needed to remember what he could do, and I needed to remember I could do this as well.

Riding horses and living faith are constantly asking me to learn, to remember what I know, and to learn more. Sometimes I just want the gold star, to say I've learned enough, so I can ride the calm horse that doesn't need to learn anything new.

Except that's not faith. That's complacency, and in faith and riding, that's what gets you stuck. And I felt that steady presence of God, settling on my soul like the crop on Fatimo's shoulder, communicating that yes, this is the way it's going to be.

Not better or worse, but different. A shift to a new way. The arena is a place where this shifting, this learning, this finding a new way happens. It's where I ride and learn, about horses and myself. It is the place where riding, faith, and work combine in a relationship deep with dimension. The arena is the place where I learn about God because I am in the arena, working, failing, succeeding, and riding horses. It is a place of hard work and valuable insights, a holy container for the great acts that are us living our faith.

CHAPTER 7
Excessive Weight

*N*o one is at our best emotional selves right now," Brad said. Brad and I met our first day in seminary, more than twenty years ago. We made it through exactly one day and three hours into the next day of orientation before we escaped from the seminary close located in the Chelsea neighborhood of New York City into the immensity of the city that we yearned to become lost in. We lived down the hall from each other until we graduated, and have been essential parts of each other's souls since.

When the COVID-19 pandemic settled in, Brad and I had regular FaceTime talks. We'd seen each other each year on vacations. This year would clearly end that pattern.

I sipped on my gin and tonic as I nodded to his comment.

I wondered about the qualifier *best,* as if there was a way to be "best" at anything in the midst of a global pandemic that had truly pulled the fibers out of the fabric we had all, in one way or another, woven together. We are just our reasonable emotional selves right now, which more than not meant frayed, stressed, and anxious.

We humans were at capacity, and another added weight, no matter how seemingly small, in most of our lives, was the drop of water that became a roaring flood that pulled us under.

Horses have a weight capacity, depending on their size. Most horse people know that a horse can carry about 20 percent of their body weight, including tack and rider. A smaller Morgan pony like our Mighty Moe at Wingswept, regardless of his bigger-than-life attitude, can carry about 180 pounds. A Friesian, one of the smaller draft horse breeds that is ridden under saddle, can carry almost 300 pounds. Too much weight on a horse during a ride and they experience elevated heart and respiration rates and stress, especially in their legs.

We have a capacity for what we can carry too. Much like horses, when we exceed our capacity, our bodies tell us in all sorts of ways. We don't sleep well. Our heart rates and respiration rates increase. We often engage in unhelpful coping mechanisms. Our emotions settle very close to the surface and, at least with me, feel like they are pushing against the inside of my skin to find a way, any way, to escape. Or we push our emotions down deeper into our souls until we can't feel them anymore when they inevitably, eventually pop out onto someone else when we vomit our unexplored emotions onto them, making quite the mess.

What I realized on this particular Tuesday afternoon, after talking with Brad, is that I had not only reached my capacity, but I had exceeded it several emotional stones ago and my body and soul decided to stop the trail ride and park out. We were not moving another inch.

Global pandemics, paired with the reality of life as a human, exceed our capacity. For me, the anxiety and stress of being a pastor of a church in the time of COVID-19 was more than enough to exceed the weight I could carry. All the scientific health protocols suggested that gathering in person inside in a familiar worship space, singing out loud, and hugging each other was dangerous. What, then, did church now look like?

Added to that weight was watching the reality of hundreds of thousands of people dying, alone, because of this pandemic. People were worried about their jobs. Adults with children at home were suddenly given the additional task of teaching online. Relationships were reaching capacity without the release of time away. Neighbors were living with serious health issues and worried if they would ever be able to do something as mundane as shop for groceries in person again.

When I am at capacity, I don't heed the wisdom of horses and stop. I keep going.

Until I can't, and then I fall down in a crushed heap of a shambled mess. I've lost the ability to distinguish between what weight is mine to carry and what weight has been thrown on me by people who don't want to carry their own stuff. I almost always have some stuff that I picked up along the way because surely someone has to carry it. So I sit in the rubble and too often feel like I want to cry, but the debris of it all blocks any flow of tears.

Where do we go to leave the excess weight, to cry until we find some equilibrium in our souls between air and water, spirit and substance? How do we rediscover what is ours to carry and what weight we have picked up that needs to be dropped until the person who needs to carry it comes along?

In this not-my-emotional-best-self place, I didn't have an answer to these questions, so I went to ride because that is what I do on most Wednesday nights. Spencer is a show horse who retired early. I am not too much weight for him, but I was too much weight for me. We did not have a good ride.

"You're overthinking it," one of the other riders offered as I simply couldn't get Spencer to trot. I've been getting horses to trot for years. Walking is sometimes a challenge. Cantering may be challenging as well, depending on the horse. But getting a horse to trot?

I can get a horse to trot,

But I couldn't get Spencer to trot today.

I took Spencer into the middle of the arena and stopped. Maybe, I thought, if I could get myself to take a breath, I could ride. Alyssa, that night's instructor, let me stand with Spencer for a bit, then told me, "Go back out and ride."

I wanted to sit on him in the middle of the arena and cry, which just made me madder. Why now? Why, after hours and days and weeks and months of all this pressure, is today the day when too much weight decides to make a mess of things? Why could it not have been last night, at home, or anywhere else?

I grudgingly walked Spencer out to the rail. After another few messy attempts, I finally asked him clearly enough, and he picked up his trot. Spencer and I rode together for another forty-five minutes. He carried me and all my weight into some semblance of a ride. We trotted and cantered and walked, but none of the gaits felt easy, and not because I was overthinking my riding, but because the excessive weight of too much of life meant my mind and spirit and soul were anywhere but sitting on Spencer. After an ugly ride, I took him into his stable and stripped him of his tack. I kept on my sunglasses in the stall because I was one molecule of oxygen settling on my soul away from every tear bursting forth that had been dammed up over the past months.

A quick brush of Spencer, and I walked with a lock-jawed purpose to the yearling paddock, situated near the front of the farm and far away from all the other people on this Wednesday evening. Arya, who I've watched grow from a skinny newborn into the full-blooded warrior princess for which she's named, nickered at me. I walked to the fence, and she came to see if I had treats.

I did, and I handed her a mint. She let me reach out and rub her neck, and I simply wept. The weight of all that I'd been carrying pushed me into the fence so I could let weathered wood bear some of my weight. I still wore my sunglasses as the sun set, and I sobbed while I nuzzled Arya. The COVID-19 pandemic had made physical touch between those of us not in the same households potentially dangerous, and in the moment, I hadn't realized how much weight that aloneness added. Arya, perhaps, did. She's not one to stand still, but tonight she did until I cried myself into a slow trickle of tears. I just stood there, my hands resting on her neck, feeling her warmth, her presence. She nuzzled me a bit as I finally found a deep breath, the first one I think I'd taken in weeks. I found stillness, and she stood there with me, sharing some of my weight.

Horses are made to carry weight. So are humans. But we aren't made to carry too much for too long. Sometimes, the response to the excess isn't to drop it all, but to find those moments where God shows up to remind us of what we need to hold, what we need to leave, and what wasn't ours to pick up in the first place.

And sometimes, I don't have to carry any excessive weight at all. I simply have to stand and cry and love a horse.

CHAPTER 8

The Space in Between

❧

*J*onah is a petty, annoying, and exasperating prophet, which is exactly why I love his story so much. The book of Jonah in the Hebrew Bible is a jewel of an example of God's grace for us humans in all our disobedience, whining, and downright pettiness, so spectacularly embodied by Jonah. I adore the book of Jonah.

Jonah, we read, is a prophet of the Lord and is called by God to go to Nineveh to tell them to get right with God . . . or else. Jonah, naturally, does the exact opposite, makes all sorts of choices that communicate his complete abdication of this holy call, and ends up in the belly of a great fish, where he suddenly becomes a remarkably eloquent and faithful person, singing the Song of Jonah:

> I called to you, O God, out of my distress, and you answered
>   me;
> out of the belly of Sheol I cried, and you heard my voice.
> You cast me into the deep, into the heart of the seas,
> and the flood surrounded me; all your waves and billows
>   passed over me.
> Then I said, "I am driven away from your sight;

how shall I ever look again upon your holy temple?"
The waters closed in over me, the deep was round about me;
weeds were wrapped around my head at the roots of the
   mountains.
I went down to the land beneath the earth,
yet you brought up my life from the depths, O God.
As my life was ebbing away, I remembered you, O God,
and my prayer came to you, into your holy temple.
With the voice of thanksgiving, I will sacrifice to you;
what I have vowed I will pay, for deliverance belongs to the
   Lord!
(Jonah 2:2–7, 9)[6]

Humans have a long tradition of suddenly becoming the best followers of God ever when we find ourselves in the belly of a fish or other similar messes that are the results of our own poor life choices.

In response to his newly found obedience, Jonah gets vomited out on the beach, and God again tells Jonah to go to Nineveh, which this time he does, and Nineveh repents. Jonah is completely annoyed by this and angry at God. God causes a castor bean plant to grow over Jonah to shade him in his anger. Jonah is happy about this turn of events, but then God causes an east wind to blow, which kills the plant.

And Jonah is angry again. Furious, in fact. So angry he'd rather die than live. God asks something along the lines of, "Let me get this right, you are this angry about the castor bean plant, that you didn't do anything to grow?"

Jonah says yes.

God continues: "You are concerned about the bush, for which you did not labor and which you did not grow; it came into being in a night and perished in a night. And should I not be concerned about Nineveh, that great city, in which there are more than a hundred and twenty thousand persons who do not know their right hand from their left, and also many animals?" (Jonah 4:10–11).

And the story ends. No pages stuck together or suggestion that another scroll has a neat conclusion where Jonah realizes he is being a jerk. Nope.

The book of Jonah doesn't end with a resolution. The text ends with a question from God, a rhetorical one, I suspect, but we're not completely sure. The book ends with Jonah and us, as readers, in liminal space.

The term comes from the Latin *limen*, meaning "threshold." In the world of faith and spirituality, it is broadly used to speak of being in a time of transition, when we've moved from something but have not yet reached the new something. Liminal space is the hallway we enter after we walk out of one room where something of our old life inhabits, but we're not sure where we go next.

Liminal space is certainly rich with possibilities and hopes, but it's also scary and unsettling. Hope lives there because God is in liminal space, but it is, by definition, a place of transition. Calling liminal space *transition* is a bit kind. In many transitions, I have some idea of what may be coming, even if it's just a broad idea. But with liminal space, I have no idea what is really next. I'm walking through the wilderness at night and I can hear wildness moving all around me. I don't have a flashlight. And I have to go to the bathroom.

Liminal space, spiritually speaking, is truly stepping out from the known or, in most cases, being shoved out the door of what we have known and with which we have become comfortable, and stumbling, falling, and crashing for a while. We are moving from something to something else, and the something else is almost completely unfamiliar and even, perhaps, unwelcome. If we are fortunate, we have a vague idea of what the something else is. Most times, though, we don't. We are, like Jonah, trying to turn around to the direction of the familiar while God keeps sending storms and winds and big fish to move us to the unfamiliar.

Liminal space is necessary for life; it's inescapable even. We will all be shoved from the room we've gotten just the way we wanted it into the hallway filled with nothing. The death of someone we love throws us into liminal space. An unexpected crisis, children growing up, parents getting older, relationships not working out: when these events knock on our doors and we open the door to see who's there, we are pulled through the doorway into liminal space. We have to transition. Otherwise we stay stuck in one place, one groove, one speed.

I can appreciate the desire to stay stuck. On many days, when my not-barn life has been filled with too much wandering and uncertainty that is life, I've had many lessons where I've climbed into my saddle and wished I could just walk my horse at a slow, ambling gait. My seat could drop deeply into the saddle, my hips could rock with the movement, and my feet could dangle, free from the stirrups. Depending on the horse, I may or may not hold the reins.

Except, while that's technically riding a horse, sitting on a horse at a walk is not fully riding a horse. So, at some point, no matter my personal mood of the moment, my instructor will tell me to trot.

For the briefest moment (or sometimes longer, depending on the horse), we are in liminal space. We are leaving behind the walk and moving into the trot or rack or canter. We are in between—not where we were, but not what we will be.

Transitions in riding take work. I've done entire lessons where I've done nothing but work on transitions. As I move from the walk to the canter, am I lifting up or leaning forward? Are my hands relaxed, so my horse has enough slack on the reins to go forward, or pulling backward, a sure message to the horse not to go anywhere? Am I calling for the gait I want with confidence or cautiousness, the latter of which almost inevitably causes confusion? Have I placed the horse well in the ring so she has plenty of space in front of her to go forward?

And what is my body doing? Am I firm in my core or am I clenched and tight? Am I, as the rider, settled down and sitting up? Downward transitions particularly—from the trot or canter to the walk—often cause a rider to fall forward and lose balance. Reins go slack and feet move backward. And that's when you can fall.

Knowing the horse is helpful too. Some horses transition slowly. We call for the new gait, and they respond, but they need, as I recognize, a longer runway to start and stop. Expecting them to start and stop immediately is unhelpful and unrealistic. But I need to prepare for what I want them to do and give them the tools they need.

A few horses, Rose in particular, transition quickly, particularly from a canter to a walk. She hits the brakes. Suddenly. And if I'm not ready, I will be abruptly tossed forward onto her neck, grabbing pieces of her blond mane to stay on. Slower transitions, quite honestly, are easier to maneuver than sudden ones. In riding and in life.

My instructor, during a transition-only lesson, once asked me to transition with my body first before using my voice.

In saddle-seat riding, we talk to our horses. And they mostly listen. While clicks and kisses aid us as we call for the trot or the canter, the horses are also quite good at understanding our words. Horses, however, speak primarily through feel. They feel our bodies before they hear us.

The look on my face conveyed my doubt in this particular teaching method.

"Trust me. Just let your body tell the horse what you want. Don't use your words," she urged.

So I did. After a few turns around the ring at different gaits, she called me over to discuss the practice. Then, I said, "Slowing down was easier, from the trot or canter to the walk."

She nodded, not surprised. "Because you sat deeply in the saddle and focused on staying centered."

"But waiting for the horse to get the trot and then posting definitively feels more secure," I noted. It also helped the horse I was riding know this was, indeed, the gait I wanted.

Transitions on horses have some general guidelines, but they don't follow a strict set of rules. Noah, Izzy, and CLo need me to wait until they pick up the trot for sure before I start posting. They can feel my body say, "Yes," to the gait I wanted. Amy and Maria toss me up into a post quickly and are right there, ready to go. Glory always looks for an excuse to stop cantering, while Tipitina is flawless in the canter and I simply need to stay centered.

But in that space, in that liminal space, so much is going on between horse and rider. We say words, we make sounds, we push in with legs and loosen up reins and quickly take them back up, and we shift and settle in the saddle. Steph, my instructor, points out that the difference between an accomplished rider and a beginner is often seen in transitions.

Transitions between gaits require attention, tiny movements, and some certainty that the transition is as important as the end result.

Jonah is a book of transitions, of God finding Jonah in liminal space and inviting him to journey into more liminal space. The direction Jonah wants to go is counter to the direction God nudges him. Jonah's adventures end with him still in a place of uncertainty, of transition, of liminal space.

Our faith is too often a quest for sure and certain, and our movements between places of stability are regarded in a pejorative sense. "I feel so . . . unsettled," we say when we're unsure and lacking. Yet, the stories of our faith, particularly in the Bible, are mostly people being unsettled, moving between places and finding God in a different, even fresh way during the transitions.

Before riding and before a few of my own journeys that resemble Jonah's fleeing from God and ending up covered in fish vomit while seething, I saw transitions as just a way to get from one place to another.

A deeper faith and years of riding have embodied the truth that transitions are as important, if not more so, than the settled places. They are where we move and shift. They are where I grow and change. Transitions test my muscles and my focus. They are where God moves me to slow down or speed up or just change the way I'm moving to better be present to whatever God is calling me to do.

Feel it with my body. Then talk. Then shift.

CHAPTER 9
Monsters in the Corners

$\mathscr{H}$orses are many things, but unswervingly brave is not one of them—not, at least, in the way we usually think of being brave.

Horses are exquisite and impressive. They evoke awe and some sense of wildness when we watch them run across a meadow, their flowing manes and tails adding to the visual elegance of their powerful movements. Hearing a herd of horses gallop across a field is certainly intimidating, and more than one person has used the word *majestic* to describe the horse.

But brave?

Well, maybe in their own peculiar ways. The bravery of horses is intricately mixed with a quirky dynamism and liveliness from eons of being a prey animal. As a mammal that is on the lower rungs of the food chain, a horse with fearless bravery that stands nose to nose with a predator does not usually ensure longevity for this particular horse. At a sign of trouble or potential danger, horses choose to flee. That response has allowed them to survive for eons.

Horse breeds do differ in temperament, and temperament varies among individual horses due to many of the same environmental factors that influence human temperament.

Quarter Horses tend to be easygoing, even docile. Morgan horses are a bit spunkier, but still eager to please. One of our resident Morgan horses at the farm, Mighty Moe, has a spunky attitude that is a 60-40 mix of cooperative and headstrong. Which part is 60 percent and which part is 40 percent can vary on any given day, and he's one of my favorites to ride.

Saddlebreds aren't amazingly skittish, but they are very aware of things. This hyperawareness makes them particularly suited for the show ring, thus their moniker as the peacocks of the horse world. Their ears are pricked, listening to all the sounds. Their eyes are focused. They are paying attention to their surroundings in the exacting way Saddlebreds do. American Saddlebreds, with their attitude and their beauty, were featured in several films of the Golden Age of Hollywood. *National Velvet,* one version of *Black Beauty,* and *Mr. Ed* all featured Saddlebreds (Mr. Ed was half Saddlebred). Saddlebreds are spirited. Saddlebreds are stunning. But I wouldn't always call them brave.

Breed experts note that the Kentucky Saddler, a recent precursor to the modern American Saddlebred, was the horse of choice for several officers during wars, including General U. S. Grant, whose horsemanship was the stuff of legend.

As CLo jumped sideways and began to move backward as we headed into the corner of the inside arena on our ride today, I wondered how anyone rode Saddlebreds into battle. I mean, yes, I'm aware that over a century and a half of breeding has an impact. But CLo is scared of monsters in the corner of the indoor arena. Fatimo is nervous about doors. Lily is terrified of Styrofoam and George the Donkey (although her terror is selective depending on the day and her rider). And Spencer is unsettled by pitchforks.

CLo, whose full name is Crazy Love, came to Wingswept several years ago as the project horse of a woman who decided to give up her project. She tried to train her, including a failed attempt to get CLo to slow gait and rack. Those gaits are not guaranteed in every Saddlebred. The ability of a horse to slow gait and rack has much to do with conformation, how they are put together physically. Sort of the same way humans are better suited for particular sports based on how tall or how short they are.

My first ride on CLo was to get her to flat walk all the way around the arena. Over ninety minutes later, we accomplished the goal. Both of us were sweaty and exhausted. Part of training CLo into the lesson program was helping her learn what we wanted her to do, being clear when we asked her to do something, and rewarding her when she did it. Because she hadn't finished her training, she often just ran through every way she knew how to move when we asked her to trot or canter or flat walk, including a few mystery gaits.

When she did get her trot or her canter, I petted her and scratched her neck and told her what a good girl she is. I still do. Positive affirmation works for horses. In the midst of my mini lovefests on her, she got the name Sweet C from me. I showed her at her very first show, a winter tournament, which is less formal than the shows during spring, summer, and fall show seasons, and she excelled. Most importantly, she flat walked every time I asked her to flat walk. I like to think that because of that show, my friend and fellow rider Stuart decided to buy her.

It probably wasn't, but we need positive reinforcement too.

CLo has remained part of our lesson program. She is gentle and kind and has a canter that is collected and smooth. Her canter has a precise way of providing a gentle massage to my lower back that often gets tight and sore from life and being older. She can't trot over a corn cob, but her job isn't to have a high-stepping trot. Her job is to teach riders to ride.

And one way she teaches riders is with her tendency to not be brave.

CLo is much braver than she used to be. I rode her for one entire summer when the back fence of the arena was simply so scary for her she refused to stay on the rail, as we say. I negotiated with her, and we rode about three feet off the rail when we went by that stretch of the arena, with enough space between her and the fence line that she didn't want to jump sideways. She has since become brave enough to go right next to all the rails in the outside arena.

Our inside barn is a bit different. The corners are scary, as is the heater when it blows in the winter. Sometimes the specific way the footing has been dragged adds to the possibility of terror. Her response is to shy away from the thing or sometimes to jump. She doesn't escalate her fear by tearing off into a gallop, but she does, in her own way, teach riders to be aware, to ride with our thighs and seat firmly on the saddle, and to remember we are in partnership with a living thing who has her own ideas.

Today, CLo's ideas were completely focused on the door that was open for some reason. Maybe it was being painted or maybe someone just left it open. CLo didn't care about the reason. She just cared that it was different, and different for her is scary, and that meant she needed to shy and jump when we rode by it.

After the third trip around, with me calming her with my words and guiding her closer to the open door, I wondered aloud to my instructor Alyssa how on earth CLo's cavalry horse ancestors rode into battle with cannon explosions and people running in every direction, with smoke from all the artillery creating an almost impenetrable haze. She, in her precious Sweet C charm, is startled by an open door of the indoor arena. I can only imagine her reaction to the sounds of a battle.

I turned CLo in a circle and steadily talked to her as we picked up our trot again. I pushed her forward with my legs, telling her what a brave girl she was and how the corner with the open door was safe, all in the voice tone that we heard as children when we skinned our knees after a tumble on the sidewalk and our parents, grandparents, or some adult who we were sure knew how to save the world reminded us we would be okay as they carefully placed a bandage on our wounds and kissed them.

This time, she only spooked slightly, but we made it through the corners of the far end of the indoor arena safely. At the other end, I called her down to the walk and rubbed her neck, reminding her again what a good, brave girl she had been to face down the monsters in the corners.

Horse are herd animals and prey animals. Their natural state is with other horses in a herd to have protection. Safety is indeed in numbers for horses. They have evolved over the eons, like all creatures, to ensure survival. From the way their vision works to the sensitivity of their skin, horses are almost hyperaware of their surroundings, which means they are more adept at noticing changes and more responsive to changes. Just in case that change may be a carnivore looking for a meal, flight wins over fight.

A newly opened door registers to CLo as a change in the space that is different and possibly dangerous. Add to that the way she is already a bit skittish inside, and she decides to do the one thing she can to feel safe—jump away from it and flee.

My job as her rider is to remind her she is safe. I don't do that by being skittish myself, but by being the rider. As my instructor said once, riding teaches you to remain calm in the face of potential catastrophe because only one of you at a time gets to freak out and it's never your turn.

But sometimes I do need to freak out. I need to jump and run at the sight of the monsters, the way the ground has shifted under my feet and the light makes things look too different. Sometimes I don't need to be brave. Sometimes, I don't want to be brave. Sometimes, in the midst of monsters, I need to flee.

We tell stories of the saints in Christianity and their bravery in the face of persecution, hardship, and death. Constance and her fellow nuns bravely stayed in Memphis, Tennessee, in 1878 when most of the population fled to escape the Yellow Fever pandemic. They didn't flee. They cared for those who were sick, and most of them died of the same illness as those they nursed and comforted.

Joan of Arc bravely followed God's call to lead the French army to victory. Even when she was laughed out of the French court for proclaiming she was sent by God, she didn't flee. Instead, she went back to the court and demanded an audience with the king until the king finally listened.

One of my personal favorites, Lawrence, was charged by a Roman prefect to bring the wealth of the church to him. Lawrence instead brought the poorest Romans. The prefect, unimpressed by Lawrence's word play, condemned Lawrence to be fried to death on an iron slab. Legend says Lawrence told his executioner to turn him over because he was done on one side.

Bravery with a good side of sarcasm will almost always get you named a saint or a heretic. The saints of the church, even our secular saints, are imbued with the quality of bravery, as if living life in any way that isn't brave is a failure. Life, however, is a scary place. And often, humans are going about our business when those monsters that would devour our souls appear at the edge of the meadow.

The monsters of life's randomness and uncertainty, and even the more horrid parts that are evil that too often wear the clothing of logic and popularity, make me want to run into a stall and shut the gate.

Bravery is rarely my first response. Or my second or third. Something that camouflages as bravery is often an attempt to find logic and control in a situation. Someone got cancer because of something they did, some life choice. People live in oppressive poverty in Appalachia because they choose to stay where there are few jobs, and they should just move somewhere else. Yet, with a bit of a push, that brave logic tumbles down like me when a horse jumps and spins and I'm not settled in the saddle. Environmental degradation creates cancer alleys in many states. Generational poverty inflicted by policies of corporations and governments create patterns that are almost impossible to break. The racism of centuries continues to oppress, persecute, and murder those who Jesus loves.

Another desperate reach for bravery is to convince myself the monsters aren't real. The incendiary words of leaders, both civic and religious, aren't really inviting me to hate my neighbor. It's just the way the light is shining on them. Monsters, however, are real. And our false attempts at bravery mute a holy response, a godly response, to them. I should jump and want to run from the evil of hate. I do get to be anything but brave. I even get to be cowardly, and that is a holy response.

Peter knew this. Peter was imbued with the quality of bravery, the one who was named as the rock on whom Jesus would build the church. Peter was the brave, faithful first bishop of Rome in church lore.

Except that he was not brave. Peter was more foolhardy and cowardly than brave. Before his crucifixion, Jesus told Peter that he would deny he even knew Jesus. Peter, full of that false belief that bravery is the only holy response, insisted Jesus had lost his mind.

"Right. Well, before the cock crows, Peter, you'll deny me," Jesus responded.

When I visited Jerusalem, one thing I noticed is that the roosters crow all day, at almost every hour. Jesus's response to Peter's declaration of bravery and unwavering faith is, "Peter, when you find yourself afraid and in danger, you're going to fold like a cheap lawn chair."

Jesus knew Peter so well; he knew that Peter would not be brave. Yet, filled with that knowledge of Peter's spectacular lack of bravery, Jesus named Peter the rock on whom Jesus would build his church.

Jesus seems to value honest cowardice, fear, and faintheartedness more than our responses of bravado, perhaps because these responses to all that is scary in life are real and unvarnished and truthful. Bravery may make for good stories, but cowardice makes space for us to try again. Cowardice makes space for us to ask God for help.

CLo did try again when I urged her forward, past the scary open door in the inside arena and the back fence in the outside arena and all the scary things she encountered. We have developed a relationship, this kind mare who isn't brave, and I who also am not brave. She trusts me, and I trust her.

Holy bravery is embodied in both horses and the saints, the created beings of God who feel the very deeply rooted response to flee in light of danger and often do exactly that when we are faced with something new, disturbing, and unsettling. Life is scary because on a regular basis, we encounter the monsters in the corners. And, if we're honest, we flee (or want to).

The bravery of the saints and horses listens to the voice that coaxes them forward into whatever is scary or seems scary. And they trust that voice.

Maybe the bravery of horses is the bravery God offers us: not the stoic, never-flinch kind, but bravery that notices, that jumps, and takes the time to feel God coaxing us forward into whatever act of bravery and love we are called to do.

CHAPTER 10
Working Too Hard

---

*Y*ou're working harder than he is!" I heard my instructor Stephanie yell as Moe and I took the straightway.

She was right. Horses, most of them anyway, are no fools. Why work harder than they have to during a lesson? Do just enough, and see if that works. Or, in Moe's case, do a bit less than enough.

Moe is my favorite Morgan pony. He has all sorts of feisty spirit. Pony is a specific designation related to height at their withers, the ridge between a horse's shoulder blades. A pony generally stands under 14.2 hands (about fifty-eight inches) at the withers, but different breed organizations have different uses of the term. Morgan horses are solidly built and easy keepers, meaning they stay at a healthy weight with little effort. The Morgan horses I know are powerful and personable.

Moe fits that description. He's compact and chubby, but he's a fit chubby. I love riding him because he can trot like a little rocket and canter slower than other horses walk. His strength and personality have earned him the nickname Mighty Moe.

I love him because his neck is ticklish and he shivers all over when it's touched. I love him because he flattens his ears in annoyance or disgust at random things, from one of us walking by him to the way a butterfly lands on the fence where he's standing. I love him because he will decide he'd like to get a nosh of grass during a lesson and take a rider right to the center of the outdoor arena so he can get a snack of green grass.

Quirks make humans and horses more enjoyable.

Moe is also an excellent teaching horse for beginners. Despite his salty sassiness, he is also remarkably patient and calm with beginning riders. Or maybe he just enjoys that beginning riders don't ask too much of him, so what looks like patience is a good nature mixed with a dash of laziness.

I am not a beginning rider, although I have days when I wonder. Tonight, however, I am riding Moe, and he and I are negotiating his energy level. He's tossed his head a couple of times when I've suggested, gently at first and firmly thereafter, that I'd like his head up and not level with his body. I've clucked him forward, and he's going, but still with that dash of lazy. I'm waiting for Moe to decide to get his engine going forward. At the moment, he's still considering my request.

Posting a trot is moving with the rhythm of the horse at her trot, a two-beat gait where opposite pairs of the horse's legs move forward at the same time. That movement causes the rider to bounce with the gait. Posting, a controlled rise from the saddle and an equally controlled lowering back into the saddle, allows the rider to have balance and discipline over our own bodies and helps us communicate to the horse. The post also helps the pressure on the horse's back. When a rider posts, they aren't bouncing all over the horse's back, but instead rising and falling with the movement of the horse. Posting makes a ride at a trot considerably more comfortable for both rider and horse.

The key to a post is the down motion. The natural movement of the horse bounces me up out of the saddle, and I use the muscles in my thighs and core and my balance to ease back into the saddle. This happens pretty quickly, almost imperceptibly, after years of riding.

Posting was perceptible when I first began riding. I did lots of counting: one–two–one–two. Up–down–up–down as I allowed my body to feel the horse's movement and respond to it. Learning to post inevitably means making mistakes. My hands should be still, not going up and down with my body, confusing the horse with all the strange pressure I'm putting on the reins. Beginning riders tend to double bounce with the post when we sit a bit too long in the saddle and almost work against the horse's natural movements.

The post is a movement really from the knees to the waist, so my lower leg should be fixed in the stirrups, not moving around to give me momentum or to use my feet to push me up. Let the horse do that, Stephanie would say. The post, as well as sitting the canter, should look still and effortless for the rider, even though we are using all kinds of muscle movement to have the illusion of stillness, even when we are posting a trot.

The height of my post (how far I rise out of the saddle) depends on how lofty the horse is. *Lofty* is a term we use to talk about the bounce a rider gets out of the saddle when the horse trots. Nina does not have a lofty trot. Hers is gentle and smooth, mainly because she's short-strided (her legs don't move far apart from each other when she trots). Nina's trot is so gentle at times I barely leave the saddle when I post.

Noah, at the opposite end of the spectrum, will bounce me to the moon and back with his trot. He's a big boy with long legs and substantial movement when he goes forward. His forward motion is still a bit unnerving to me when I ask him to trot, until I remember I can indeed post his trots. Noah's lofty trots also mean my legs will be sore the next day. Always.

Moe's is a good medium. But with that dash of lazy he has tonight, I'm actually doing more lifting myself out of the saddle on the upbeat than riding his bounce upward. I'm working harder than he is.

Stephanie reminds me of that again when we come around on that side of the arena where she's instructing us tonight. "Don't work so hard," she repeats.

Riding horses is a relationship that depends on communication. There's constant communication between horse and rider, between Moe and me. I wiggle my reins to get his head up. When he responds, I give the reins a bit, my telling him that his head is where I want it. If I want him to go off the rail, I push my leg in to indicate that. He responds, moving away from the pressure. To encourage him to up his energy level, I give him a tap from both of my legs on his sides and even a tap with my crop. He picks up his energy (which may not necessarily mean he goes faster) and we move together.

The relationship of riding is a precise kind of equality that makes horse and rider move with each other, not against each other. I can't make Noah trot gently. It's not who he is. So my job as his rider is to be controlled and centered in my post, to create that measured stillness with my movements and even my lack of any unnecessary ones, to help him trot his best.

Moe needs a bit more energy, but I don't get that from him by doing his work for him. I do that by doing my work for me and communicating for him to step up. He's capable of more energy. I know that. He knows that. As long as I'm working too hard, carrying more than my share, why should he work? Moe is no fool.

I, however, can be.

I can't do his work. I can do my work. And my work is to still my hands, so I'm not using them to pull myself out of the saddle. My work is to push out my legs and roll in my knees, so my feet and lower legs stay still. My work is to let Moe's movement lift me out of the saddle, then control my fall so I sit gently until I lift again.

My job is to do my work. Not Moe's. Not someone else's. But how many times have I thought or even said aloud, "It's just easier if I do it," when I realize I'm doing someone else's work.

Maybe it is. When I'm helping a new rider at the barn learn how to tack up and untack a horse, I would absolutely be faster taking off a bridle and brushing the horse. But speed is not the goal. The goal is for others to learn the basic skills of caring for the horses they are riding and to develop relationships with the horses they are grooming. Relationships cannot be rushed.

When I take this a step further, into my own spiritual and emotional life, I'm also reminded of this truth. I can do my work, but not someone else's. I can be present to someone's fear, but I can't make them feel unafraid. I can tell someone the church loves them, but I can't make them feel loved in a faith that has often told those in certain groups they are not fully welcome. I can remind someone that grief is a completely holy response to the death of someone, but I can't make someone welcome the presence of grief.

Often, though, I work too hard. If I just suggest this book or maybe if they go to that group or try this spiritual practice, they will be okay. Maybe, but I have to be careful that I'm not working too hard and doing someone else's work, trying to make someone grieve, act, or be a way that I think they should be, no matter how well-intended that may be.

That is not love.

Horses that don't respond to the communication from their riders can be dangerous. The same is probably true for humans who don't respond to communication from other humans. Yet many of us have this idea, this concept, that if someone doesn't respond, we just have to work harder, lifting ourselves up into labor for the sake of the relationship until we've exhausted ourselves from all the work. Instead of stepping back, we gather our weariness and do more work.

I wonder if our translation of loving one another has gotten twisted into thinking we should control one another instead. This control means that we fail to recognize when the work we're doing in the relationship isn't helpful, safe, or even life-giving for either of the parties. Loving our neighbor does not mean working ourselves to exhaustion for another person. Loving our neighbor does not mean trying to meet another person's every need or telling the other person what we think they need, directly or passively.

Love means I check in with me. I control my movements and acknowledge my emotions. I do my emotional labor, not someone else's, even when that means recognizing someone will decide to take a path I think will be hurtful to them. Love allows that.

Because that is how God loves us. We have a freedom to live our lives, to make good choices and bad ones, and to know God loves us in the midst of all of them. I suspect much of the unexpressed experience of God is God saying, "This whole creation thing would just be easier if I did it."

And it would. I think of all humans have learned because love stepped back and let us try and fail and fail and fail some more. I think of all I have learned because love stepped back and let me try and fail, sometimes spectacularly, and even, eventually, learn my way into confidence and some small bit of wisdom.

We have also succeeded in love. We've found our way into grace and love because we did the work. Our work.

I wonder how many human relationships God watches me engage in and tells me, "You're working harder than they are."

All relationships that span any significant length of time take ebb and flow work, but you are working too hard if a relationship rarely has any moments of ebb and all the moments of full-on white-water rapid flow. Those relationships where we are working to satisfy, adapt, or capitulate to the subtle suggestions or overt demands of the other so that we exhaust our souls, while the other person trots along at the pace they have determined, ignoring all cues and communication, are out of balance.

Or maybe we've been that other person, letting someone work too hard on us. I know I have.

I stop working too hard in my post. Moe slows down. I tap him with the crop and push my hands forward to loosen the reins a bit. Suddenly, Moe the little chubby rocket steps up. My work is on the down motion of the trot, and his is on the up motion. I can feel my legs push out from the knees, my shoulders and chest open, and my body post the way that helps me ride better and Moe trot better.

I'm doing my work. He's doing his. We are working together.

"There you go," I hear Stephanie say.

Yes, there I go. Doing my work, with God's help.

CHAPTER 11
Lounge Line Lessons

A lunge line is a long rope and sometimes two lines, usually about twenty meters, attached to the horse via the bridle or other means, that allows a person to guide the horse around in a circle, while the trainer stands in the center. It's a safe training method for young horses who are learning to be in relationship with humans as they learn words and cues of various gaits. Lunging exercises horses. Very energetic horses get lunged to get some wiggles out before being ridden. Lunging a horse is also a good way to warm up older horses before they are ridden.

The process of lunging involves a person standing in the center, and, while holding the line or lines, moving the horse around the circle, giving it time to warm up, center, and learn in a safe environment.

What's good for the horse is also good for the human.

A lunge line lesson can involve a person in the middle of the arena, keeping the horse going with the use of the lunge line, usually at a walk or a trot, freeing the rider to focus on form and balance with various exercises and drills. Some barns use this for beginner riders as they develop an awareness of balance and focus. After all, in our modern world, most of us don't grow up in the saddle. We have to learn the muscles, both physical and mental, that we need to use and strengthen to keep our legs strong, our seat firm, and our body centered and on the horse.

As it happens, our barn, thanks to an autocorrect error in the December newsletter, has recently started offering *lounge* line lessons. The adult riders quickly made the name a permanent moniker, as a special type of irony.

Because in the lessons, we do anything but lounge.

Gabrielle, our special lesson instructor who teaches bareback lessons, horsemanship lessons, and lounge/lunge line lessons, does stand in the middle, but she doesn't hold a lunge line. She teaches those of us who have ridden long enough that we are expected to be able to focus on balance and all sorts of other things while keeping the horse going forward ourselves. She stands in the middle, watching us, challenging us, coaching us, and even pointing out when we're doing a good job of not lounging in the saddle.

Over the centuries, we've developed many pieces of equipment to help us ride. The saddle gives us a firm place to sit. The tree, the solid piece of wood down the center of the saddle, is the weight-bearing point for the stirrups, giving us a place to balance with our feet. Reins connected to the bit in the horse's mouth give us a way to communicate with the horse and, if we're honest, a way to balance (although balancing on the horse's mouth with reins isn't a great habit). Bridles and girths keep reins and saddles in place on the horse. The equipment makes us feel safer because it actually makes our ride safer, for the horse and for us.

The equipment can also give us any number of ways to cheat. Stirrups that give us stability also give us a place to push up instead of letting our upper leg muscles and hips do that work. Reins provide a way to communicate direction, but they can also be a way to steady ourselves or pull ourselves up out of the saddle at the expense of the sensitivity of the horse's mouth.

In my day-to-day riding, I become attune to the routine of riding, the way I do it. My muscles develop a memory of what that way feels like. My spirit develops that same memory. That muscle and spirit memory isn't always the correct way to ride. Or maybe it was the way I could ride for a while, until my skills invite me to step up a bit and respond to my instructors' challenges—and that requires more work, more focus, and even more failure.

Sometimes, riding allows me to settle into a lazy comfort zone rather than work to reach another level of riding. Yes, my instructor will say, "You're pushing too much with your feet," to remind me I am riding the easy way, the slack way, and even the wrong way. My muscles and my mind need a shock to the system.

And there might be no better shock to the system of a rider than a lunge line lesson, especially on this December Saturday that's quite cold.

It's the week between Christmas and New Year's, when people are traveling and the barn schedule is a bit more relaxed. We've gathered, the lounge line lesson adult group, for the morning. We've all had our coffee and are catching up about various holiday adventures. We inevitably talk about the cold weather. Something about reaching a certain age means we find the weather and our various aches and pains completely engaging conversation as Gabrielle brings our horses to us.

Gabrielle has our horses ready—all the barn ponies who are a bit more game for these lessons than some of the showier horses in the barn. We pull off our heavy outer coats and complain about the cold. We're all over forty, so we again engage in the privilege of age that is complaining about the weather. We all make one more trip to the bathroom. Such is another privilege of age, I suppose.

Then we climb in the saddles and take our lounge line ponies to the rail. We're in the small barn this morning. Its smaller oval provides a perfect space for lunge line lessons. Gabrielle graciously gives us a few laps at the walk to warm up, more for the riders than the ponies.

She tells us to trot. We all pick up the trot, then after one lap, she starts the lesson in full. Gabrielle uses several drills to help us pay attention to our body in the saddle (or, on occasion, a bareback lunge line lesson, which is an entirely different adventure, especially for the inner thighs). We drop the left stirrup and post at a trot. We drop the right stirrup and do the same. This helps us notice balance. Are we centered or do we put more pressure on one side than the other? Gabrielle also helps us notice, reminding us to sit up and stay centered.

"Don't lean forward. Follow the movement of the horse," she reminds us.

"And don't fall off," one of us adds. Gabrielle smiles.

We laugh, that funny but slightly anxious laugh hoping none of us do. From the ponies, a fall would likely bruise our pride more than anything, and we certainly don't want that to happen.

She tells us to drop both stirrups. I do so and also wonder what level of madness this world of horseback riding has invited me into. I'm tossing away aids whose development made riding horses much safer. Stirrups helped riders stay on the horse more securely. But taking them away helps me realize how much of my upward post sometimes comes from my feet pushing down in the stirrups instead of my thigh muscles and core moving me up with the horse's energy. To post without stirrups means I can't cheat.

At all.

Then Gabrielle asks us to ride in two-point position.

"Without stirrups?" we all yell, incredulously.

"You can do it," she encourages.

I'm not so sure.

"Believe you can," Gabrielle says. She's a great instructor because she really doesn't give us room to doubt ourselves.

Two-point position lifts my entire seat off the saddle, so that when I have stirrups, I'm balancing through my core and knees to ride the horse's movements by putting some of my weight in the stirrups and some of my weight in my knees. I realize to do this without stirrups means I have to be hyperaware of my balance and use the strength of my thigh muscles to keep me up. So I let my morning pony partner Claira pop me up from the trot into this stirrup-less two-point position.

And I surprise myself. I can stay up. I'm not as still and steady as I am in two-point with stirrups. But I'm amazed at myself.

"Look at y'all!" Gabrielle says. I can't decide if she's excited we've accomplished this advanced drill or as shocked as we are that we managed it. We ride like this for an entire loop around the arena, after which Gabrielle mercifully calls us all down to the walk.

If you've ever wondered what holding a plank position while riding a moving pony is like, let me introduce you to the two-point position without stirrups. I make a note to find my heating pad when I get home.

Our lesson continues. We drop our reins to check our balance, noticing how we might be using the reins to pull ourselves upward. In all of this, I check to see if am I leaning forward or staying upright, with my shoulders, hips, and ankles in alignment. We sit in the saddle and do all manner of arm circles and body twists at the trot, sometimes with stirrups, sometimes without.

All of this makes us laugh at our ourselves, which on its own is a valuable lesson for adults. We all also notice things about our riding that need to be tweaked and even affirmed. Even for those of us who have ridden for some time, Gabrielle's drills show us where we've been depending too much on external equipment or noticing which muscles might need to be exercised in a different way.

Lunge line lessons also show me improvement and growth, not only where I can work to be better, but also where I have improved as a rider. I remember a time when I could barely hold a two-point position with stirrups for an entire lap around the arena. Over the days and months and years of riding, my muscles and my confidence have developed into this moment where I can indeed hold a two-point position with nothing but my balance, my leg strength, and perhaps sheer fortitude. It's not a pretty two-point position, but it counts.

After our morning lounge/lunge line lesson, Julie, another adult rider at the barn, and I are reflecting on how much fun it was, and how much we learned. We both recalled our early experiences with dropping stirrups. We are both amazed we didn't hurt the horse or kill ourselves in the early days of riding or, honestly, in our most recent lesson.

"These lessons are so good for me," Julie says. She hands me an Advil.

I agree, chasing the Advil with water from my bottle.

"It's good to have a change up for us, to work in a different way," I add.

Any lesson where we have the opportunity to pull away the aids, helps, and props that we use to see just how well or not well we are balanced, where our muscles are strong and where they can be strengthened, and what patterns we have that we think are just excellent, but in reality are not helping our movement or the horse's, is worth taking. When I can have that lesson in the midst of others who are doing the same and we're all laughing is truly a holy moment.

I wonder if I hold this same conviction for those lessons from God that come through my interactions with human relationships? Faith, like horseback riding, develops. Where I was in my faith when I was five is not the same place I was when I was eighteen, which is different from my life and faith in my fifties.

Or I hope it is.

My faith is guided by the commandment to love—to love God, my neighbor, and myself. Jesus, in the Gospel of John, shares this commandment on the night he shares bread and wine with his disciples and gives them a new commandment. He washes their feet, the act of a servant, to make his words more than words.

In some of our faith traditions, the words of our faith are amazing equipment, reaching back thousands of years and forward to our own time. These words are prayers. They are hymns. They are the worship practices that help us nourish our soul.

They are, in a very basic way, the equipment that keeps us in this relationship with God and each other. The equipment of the words of prayer balances me when I feel off-kilter. Those words help me feel more secure and even stretch me.

They can, in fact, make me too comfortable. If my entire faith is held by only the words I pray, I've let the equipment make me a bit lazy. After all, faith is not just words. Faith is what I do, how I love my neighbors—the friends I love who ride with me on cold December mornings and laugh and the people whose choices are painful to me and hurtful to others.

When faith feels hard, when I have to find a way to love a person who has deeply hurt me, I want to retreat to the words of my faith and stay there. I want to default to old habits and practices, the way the muscles of my soul have been used before. Equipment we use day in and day out for our faith— the elements of certainty that keep me fixed and perhaps even stuck: what happens when it is taken away, when we have to drop the stirrups of whatever belief we've used to balance ourselves?

Jesus likes to stand in the middle and invite me to try new muscles. Prayer is a deeply important act, and it is not the only act of faith. Jesus challenges us. Love challenges us. Love is the reason "I've never done it that way before" isn't the final response to a new way.

Lounging is not the way of Jesus. Rest might be, but staying stuck or being slothful is not. I am called to keep working, keep developing, keep noticing—all while Jesus stands in the middle and guides me, letting me work out my wiggles, my annoyances, even my failures as I continue to work in this task of love.

PART THREE
IN THE BARN

I wasn't born in a barn, but I got there as fast as I could.
—ANONYMOUS

$\mathcal{M}$y sister and I joke that my father has an extreme allergy to interstates. He's never met a back road he didn't love, often accompanied by the rationale, "It's a shortcut."

Back roads are almost never a shortcut for drive time. They are, however, shortcuts to some pieces of our country that we almost forget exist. Roads that cross rivers via covered bridges. Roads that begin as asphalt and transform into gravel and dirt, and traveling down them anoints my Subaru with red dust, a reminder of the journey. Roads that lead to the Jot Em Down store and its ilk, those places to get a soda, chips, lottery tickets, and a bologna sandwich on white bread with Duke's Mayonnaise and American cheese that always have at least two pickup trucks parked in the gravel lot.

The landscape of Kentucky is also filled with barns. You can see many from interstates and four-lane highways, but the best ones line the meandering back roads. Driving on these roads takes me past old tobacco barns that gave way to disuse when the industry faded. The gray, weathered wood barns, longer than they are wide, stand in overgrown fields, often on the tops of hills to take advantage of the breeze that would help dry the tobacco hanging from rails.

Kentucky's agricultural past and present often melds in barns built over the centuries, with additions and lean-tos to accommodate growing and changing farm tools. Mule stalls give way to tractor garages. Worn paths through tallgrass meadows are paved. Barns that once held crops and animals now hold wedding parties.

Some things do remain the same. Hay lofts still create a lovely arched roofline. Double doors stand ready to open wide for tractors, horses, and farmers to walk through. A few barns have Amish quilt squares painted on them, bright colors and geometric patterns on the front of them, above the double doors.

In the spring, bunches of renegade daffodils add color to the pale green wildness of fields that nestle barns that are no longer used and quite a few that are. Other barns take on a full life, with all manner of animals rushing in and out and through as the season comes alive. One barn that I thought was relegated to disuse surprised me when I saw goats bouncing forth one day from the doors. You can't judge a barn by its weathered wood, apparently.

Kentucky also has barns nicer than my home. The barns for the top-end Thoroughbred farms have heated floors and running water in the individual stalls. The wide barn floors are inlaid, patterned brick, or even marble. Carved and ornamented wood frames the edges of stalls. To say these high-dollar horses live better than many in Kentucky is not an exaggeration.

Then there are the four barns that are my home and sanctuary, or at least the home where my heart resides in both Nina and my barn family of the many horses who live at Wingswept Farm. The lesson barn is home base. A wooden frame is covered with a durable metal siding and roof. The main part has a wide center aisle lined with stalls on either side. Nina lives here, cozy with hay and shavings and a stall in the center of the barn so she can observe the life of the barn going back and forth.

A new addition has three more stalls and tack stalls, where we can bring the horses in who live in the field and get them ready on cushioned mat floors. The lesson barn, as do all the barns, has a hay loft where bales of hay are stacked wide and high. As a kid, I loved climbing into the hay loft of one of the many barns of friends and family and hiding away from the world with a book or my own thoughts. The smell of hay is still calming, although climbing up the ladder to the hay loft is considerably more challenging to a middle-aged woman.

Most barns also have a tack room or the variant thereof for the appropriate agricultural business. Our tack room has meticulously organized brackets for saddles and bridles, shelves for saddle pads and blankets, and cabinets for hoof grease, screwdrivers, and all the assorted items we need for riding. Saddle soap and leather conditioner are settled in nooks and crannies on the floor, often left in place from the task of conditioning all the tack, until someone comes in at the end of the day and replaces tops and puts the jars in cabinets.

In the business of a day of riding lessons, horses stand, crosstied and waiting for their riders to come. Random patches of hay, leather halters, brushes, and a water bottle or two often line the wide aisle during the day. After all, barns are places of life and movement. The stillness that happens at the end of the riding day allows for all the accumulation of the day to be cleared and put away until tomorrow. Anyone walking into the lesson barn at Wingswept for the first time would see all these things.

I see the more subtle features of this holy place as well. Above the entrance to the tack room is a frame made of two horseshoes with a picture of Katadama, a beautiful and kind horse who gently taught many riders to trust horses. He loved peppermints and having his withers scratched. He died years ago, but his spirit is still in this place, reminding us of all the horses who have been loved and who have loved us in the barn.

In Nina's stall on the back wall is a small square door with a latch on the top. It was there when Steph and Chris bought the barn. We've never figured out why it's there. Nina has decided it's there to serve as a toy for her. She likes to undo the latch and open the small door, perhaps because she can. And dutifully, every time it's open, I close it. So she can open it again when I leave.

A broom and a rake hang in the smaller storage room. At the end of the day, we sweep the concrete edges between the stall doors and the center floor of all the debris of the day, then rake the center aisle of renegade hay and other detritus to form a neat zigzag pattern. They look like ordinary tools, but over the years, I've swept and raked the barn floor hundreds of times, and each time, I feel accomplished. Too often I come to the barn with my own unfinished detritus, from worrying about parishioners to seeing the anguish in the world that breaks my heart with the chaos of human love and hate. Yet, at the end of the night, after all the tack is put up and the horses are fed, I can sweep and rake, and the barn floor is clean, ready for tomorrow. That, at least, is one task that is finished and complete. That is one task I did today that has made a difference.

Barns, like humans, are diverse in their uses and appearance. Their outside, while intriguing and striking in ways they have been put together and weathered life, are not nearly as important as what they contain—walls and floors and implements and living creatures that help us work and play and love. Barns are a particular type of holy place. The barns at Wingswept are home to horses I love and part of my soul. They house the presence of God.

CHAPTER 12

Imprints

❖

I hadn't noticed the imprints in the back wall of Izzy's stall before. I'd walked into her stall, hay and shavings dusting up the air with each step I took into the emptiness of it. The dents were made by her back hooves when she kicked at someone walking by her stall too closely, when she got her grain, when the day of the week ended in a "y," or any other time she deemed worthy of a shrill whinny and an unhesitating explosion of both back legs.

Most often, what was there was a wall. But sometimes a person was the recipient, which is why Izzy was the only horse who lived in a stall who wore a halter at all times. Izzy is the only horse I would not walk behind, even when she was crosstied in her stall. She was swift and she would kick. She would also buck and enjoyed getting in the minds of her riders, convincing them they had no business telling her what to do.

And she was right. We who rode her well didn't tell her what to do. We suggested it, a casual and breezy, "Hey, it's a lovely day out in the arena. You know what would a perfect thing to do on this day? A trot."

Most of the time, Izzy, the opinionated gray mare, would comply. Sometimes she wouldn't, and the negotiations would continue. Once she knew you respected her, even perhaps loved her, she was a pleasure.

Although a cautious pleasure—Izzy did not suffer fools holding on to her reins or sitting on her back. This amazing breed of creature that has skin so sensitive they can feel a fly land on their hindquarters knew exactly who was riding her. On this day, I was the rider, and over the years, we had found our way into a relationship of love.

Izzy and I were our own Hallmark Christmas movie of love.

When we first met, I hated her, and I'm confident the feeling was mutual. She tossed her head constantly and rolled it to the side in response to the too slack reins I offered because I knew she didn't like heavy hands. I was too scared to push her up into the bridle with my reins. She enjoyed bucking at the canter start if her head was anything but straight, which too often caused me to clamp on too tightly with my legs, giving her permission to dash off. In other words, Izzy got in my head, too, and I hated riding her as a result.

I expressed this to my instructor. "We just don't get along. I just don't need to ride her. Ever." I knew there were horses and riders that don't match, and they were not paired together for lessons.

Wise instructor Stephanie took my protestation with due consideration and then had me ride Izzy at least every other week. What Steph realized is that this was not a match issue. This was a master class in horsemanship, and Izzy had something to teach me.

Week after week, as I climbed in the saddle with equal blends of fear and hope, wondering what normal people did as a hobby, Izzy and I rode together. The first rides were probably more fear than hope, but over the weeks and months

I began to get more confident in my own riding abilities. I tapped her with the crop when she insisted on repeating unhelpful behaviors. She bucked a bit, but eventually listened. I eventually began to notice Izzy was the one horse I looked forward to riding because she was a challenge.

Izzy doesn't like her neck touched, so when I rode her, I got a pass when we had to ride two-point position, a position where riders stand up in the stirrups to improve leg position and balance.

Until I didn't get a pass and cautiously and tentatively stood up, lightly placing my hands on Izzy's neck. And she kept trotting. The first few times were unsure, but eventually two-point was part of my regular ride with her.

Then, like the scene in the middle of the town square with snow falling and both people holding a cup of cocoa, I rode Izzy for an entire lesson and she was perfect. When I called for the canter and she didn't buck, I realized I wasn't surprised. I expected her not to buck. I expected her to trot and flat walk and halt and canter with minimal complaint. She did. When she nuzzled me after I pulled her bridle off to halter her, I realized she'd decided I was no longer a fool rider she had to suffer, but one who respected her. Izzy had done her job. This little mare had given me confidence as a rider as no other horse could do. Izzy gave me courage and humility. She even reminded me to laugh when I rode.

She became my favorite horse to ride before I showed in a horse show, because I knew if I could ride her, I would ride the horse I was showing with confidence. Izzy had gotten me into show form confidence by her challenges and dares. She even let me save her one day when she was crosstied in an outdoor stall and Mighty Moe had opened the door, letting himself in to eat hay. I heard her squealing. Izzy's squeal is all her own. I went to see what disagreement was going on. I shooed the intruder out of Izzy's stall and unclipped her to take her back inside when she suddenly and unexpectedly nuzzled me, breathing deeply as she rested her forehead against my shoulder.

We stood there for several minutes in this pose of gratitude. I'd rescued her from a wayward pony. She'd rescued me from believing I couldn't ride.

Then, one day, Izzy's owners moved.

I'd ridden her on a Friday without realizing this was our last ride. She was perfect . . . for her and for me. She rolled and jerked her head as we trotted, and I gently shifted my fingers on the reins to remind her to keep her head straight. She only bucked once, and that was in response to another horse reaching over the fence trying to bite her. I completely agreed with Izzy's response to toss her hind legs out in a kick, and her lessons of sitting deep and firm meant I barely moved in the saddle when she claimed her personal space from the interloper horse. After our ride, we had our usual moments of affection as I untacked her and brushed her. And stayed away from her back legs.

But on Monday, her stall was empty.

I understand why people don't always give us notice when they leave. Goodbyes are hard. We want to believe the relationship won't change because of distance or a disruption in our routine. "We'll stay in touch," we promise each other, knowing even if we do, things will change.

Sometimes goodbyes are easier if we don't say much. In this case, Izzy's owners texted after the fact to say, "We're moving! Our horses are going with us and we will miss everyone," followed by several heart emojis.

I looked at the text again and took a deep breath, smelling hay and Izzy, who'd boarded a horse trailer a few hours earlier that day to move. I stood for a few more moments in her empty stall, tracing the imprints of the horse who became the wise and exacting teacher I needed. In a few hours, a new horse would claim this space, but the imprint of Izzy on me as a rider and as a person would be deep and lasting.

CHAPTER 13

Broken

*B*roken crayons may still color, but broken bridles do not guide.

After feeling my increased frustration on a straight line while trying to rack Cosmo with decreasing results, I noticed a piece of leather moving back and forth with Cosmo's movement, a piece that should not be hanging or moving. Cosmo was now trotting, so I continued to trot him around to the part of the fence where several other riders were gathered and brought him to a halt.

"Your bridle looks . . ." one of the riders started to say.

"Broken," I finished for her, holding the pieces in my right hand while my left hand held the reins. The right cheekpiece had broken, meaning Cosmo's bit was now an entertaining toy for him to fiddle with as it dangled on the left. And my reins were useless. So I grabbed a handful of Cosmo's dark, almost black, mane and clucked him forward to the barn. Cosmo listens well to his riders, so I wasn't too concerned that I was essentially riding him without much steering ability back to the barn.

Bridles are the equipment riders use to guide our horses. Usually made of leather with various buckles to adjust the leather straps for the horse's head size, the bridle is the point of attachment for the bit, the piece that goes in the horse's mouth, and the reins that give the rider the contact we need to guide and control the horse as we ride. Bridles come in many styles and adaptations, reflecting the style of riding and the level of communication needed for both horse and rider.

Bridles help control the horse's head. With the reins connected to the bridle, I can set a horse's head at the angle that looks best for our ride, I can nudge the horse to get their attention, and I can pull back if I need a quick stop. A bridle is, other than our own body, the most important way riders communicate with the horse.

A broken bridle is a serious problem, which explained my frustration with trying to get Cosmo to rack. Certain Saddlebred horses have the ability to do two additional gaits beyond walking, trotting, and cantering (which is essentially a very controlled gallop). These two additional gaits, the slow gait and the rack, are four-beat gaits. These gaits, called ambling gaits, look like a very powerful, fast walk with some noticeable pauses between when certain hooves meet the ground. Cosmo can slow gait and rack, and he's right-handed (yes, horses, like humans, have dominant sides), so when I need to remind him to pay attention to me or to slow him down so he's able to rack with more control, I nudge his right rein.

When the bridle broke, my connection with him broke as well, so he decided not to pay attention and chose to trot instead of rack. Trotting for Cosmo is easier, and without an ability to listen to me, he chose the easier way.

Broken bridles don't communicate with the horse. They are just broken. But they aren't always ready for the trash.

Since bridles are made up of so many separate pieces, when one part is broken or worn, as will happen with use and time, the leather can often be repaired. Even when a leather piece is beyond repair (as Cosmo's cheekpiece was), pieces can be stored to use as replacement parts when other bridles need throat latches, cavessons or nosebands, or cheekpieces replaced.

I held the four separate pieces of Cosmo's broken bridle, thankful he'd been such a good boy to listen to my voice and my body when all the communication through the reins literally fell apart. I also realized my own frustration at him as we took the last straight line. I was urging the rack, and he felt loose and choppy in his gait. I was working the reins for naught and getting more and more frustrated with Cosmo and with myself.

What I thought was Cosmo snubbing me, making me work harder than I wanted to work, and not doing what I wanted him to do, was really Cosmo not being able to feel me communicate with him. And, knowing Cosmo, there was also a part of him not wanting to do what I was asking him to do. He's a great horse. He can have zest and zip in his trot and rack when he's excited about life, but he's also got a good lazy streak after he's decided he's worked enough for the day.

Brokenness does that—stops our ability to communicate, hear, and respond. We often shut down in our broken places, stop hearing that an alternative exists from the parts of our souls that have been snapped and crushed by life, by the recklessness and even the brokenness of other humans we encounter.

We are broken by the hate we encounter from others—the messages we hear that our gender makes us less than, that aspects of our selves are fodder for jokes, that the differences in our ethnicities are to be feared instead of celebrated, that our skin colors permit knees on our necks, or that our poverty is a thing we deserve. This hate tells us we don't belong, we aren't enough, and that the leftover scraps of life and dignity we receive are indeed plenty, so don't ask for more. Our society, our families, and, sadly, even our faith communities see our broken pieces and shake their heads as they throw us wholly onto the ash heap, deeming us trash, refuse, and garbage.

Jesus was a fan of rooting around the ash heap of humanity for the treasures we've tossed. The Gospels are filled with stories of him meeting people in their brokenness, from those whose physical states of being meant they were excluded from the boundaries of community and left at the margins to fend for themselves to those whose brokenness was wrapped up in pride and superiority or titles, ranks, and riches and caused them to be fearful of anything different. Jesus held those broken pieces and saw value in them. They could be repaired and healed. They could be put to a different use. They were not garbage to God. They were valuable.

We are valuable, even in our brokenness. Especially in our brokenness.

I came to Wingswept a bit broken, literally and spiritually. I was still healing from a fall from my horse, Nina, a few months earlier, which resulted in several rib breaks, a punctured lung, and a night's stay in the hospital. Physical breaks hurt us spiritually as well. I wondered if I should even be riding. After all, riding horses is not without risk.

I'd come to Lexington broken as well. I'd served a church previously where I was subjected to words and actions that were demeaning and crushing to me as a woman, and when I expressed my discomfort with them, the head priest told me that I needed to learn how to take a joke. I could either fit in or leave, but if I left, the fact that I left would be well communicated throughout the church, so good luck getting a job.

My soul was broken, but I had just enough strength to leave. Maybe I had just enough desperation to leave. I did find another job at a church in Lexington that was a bit broken, too, from their past traumas. We shared our stories of being broken. Those stories are important, to remember that brokenness isn't a sin. Brokenness happens because life happens.

Jesus's ministry shows over and over how interested he is in those who recognize brokenness as a place God is present. Too often, we believe that brokenness is a sin, and we must continually repeat the lie that we aren't broken and never have been. That, I suspect, is the challenge, to recognize our brokenness, the ways we aren't whole, the places we've been cracked and even crushed by life and by others and to offer our brokenness to God.

We do this by telling our stories. We show the wounds, when doing so is safe, or as safe as possible. Maybe we touch the scars as we realize they are healing. My accident on Nina happened outside. She spooked when a horse kicked her, and I went into a fence. I remember thinking I'd never ride outside again.

We aren't always our most logical when our wounds make our decisions.

Until one day I realized I was riding outside again, without fear. I don't even remember how my instructor Stephanie helped me heal that broken place. Healing, I've learned, often comes softly into our lives. But on this day, riding Tipitina, who is always amazing with her powerful trot and elegant canter, I was outside and loving it.

Now I love riding outside and am one of the chief complainers when we have to go to the indoor arena, which is spacious and heated and good. But it isn't outside. Short of mud, ice, and cold that isn't good for the horses, I will add layers to ride outside.

Jesus is also a healer, and when we submit to the love of God in healing, we realize that idolizing our brokenness is not the best practice. Healing is godly too. I have continued to heal. The church I serve has continued to heal. Brokenness is part of our story, but not the only part. Our healed brokenness guides us, even helps us listen to God in a new and different way—not as someone sure and certain, but with a grace-filled humility that imbues us with empathy. As people broken and healed, we have a place, an important place, in this life with God to share the good news of love's healing.

Cosmo nudged me as I held the pieces of his broken bridle, not perfect, but still useful. He was suggesting I remember that he would like to be brushed and put into his stall for the night. I also suspect he wanted a good rubdown and a treat.

I put his broken bridle on the hook where it would be cleaned and repurposed. I led Cosmo into his stall and watched him rub his face against the edge of a doorway to scratch his face. I stood in the moment. Riding with a broken bridle could have been a moment of unbridled fear. Instead, love, healing, and horses had gotten me to a place where even a broken bridle was helpful and whole, in its own way.

CHAPTER 14

Remember the Sabbath

Mondays are my Sabbath day. For the first five years of my ordained ministry, Monday was my day off. I found a lovely rhythm of working on Sunday, then allowing the setting sun on the day of Resurrection to indicate a resetting of time for me. Turn off the phone. Sleep a little later. Spend a day reading books for pleasure or watching DVDs (back when DVDs were the primary way to watch a movie). The library in Mobile, Alabama, had a stellar collection of British television shows that were free to check out. Most Mondays meant an hour walk on the grounds of the Visitation Monastery that was next door to where I lived. My dog and I walked among magnolias and azaleas and the spirit of Christ that infused that place.

Remembering the Sabbath isn't only about worship, although that is an absolutely foundational part. Sabbath is also a time of engaging in humility, a time when I remember the world will indeed go on without my work. I can stop for a length of time and be with God. I can remember life is not only about accomplishment, but about presence. Faith is not only about working with God, but also about being with God. Rabbi Abraham Joshua Heschel in his book *The Sabbath* said,

"There is a realm of time where the goal is not to have but to be, not to own but to give, not to control but to share, not to subdue but to be in accord."[7]

Mondays were that realm of time for years.

Then I took a job at another church in Louisiana. The head priest enjoyed routinely changing all the days off of his assisting clergy. In three years, I had my day off changed seven times. And it was never on Monday.

One of the first things I did when I arrived at St. Michael's was to reclaim Monday as my Sabbath realm. Doing so felt like sliding into those old, comfortable sweatpants that wear like a warm hug. As I began giving riding more space in my life, I started riding on Mondays in addition to at least one other day during the week. Mondays are rarely crowded.

Over the years, Mondays are the days when I also enjoy just being at the barn. Alyssa instructs and challenges me as I ride. The quietness (mostly) of the barn leaves more space for being with the horses. And, as my confidence and (I hope) my skills as a rider have developed, I've moved from riding horses that improve my riding to also riding horses who might need a bit of an adjustment.

I began to observe that on Mondays, Alyssa had me ride the horses that didn't get ridden over the weekend and needed to have their wiggles worked out so that other riders feel more comfortable on them. Some horses hate Mondays as much as those humans who have to go to work after a weekend, so I get to ride them to make the transition into the week less harrowing. Mare Mondays is the phrase I use, as the mares who I adore riding are more vocal about the shift of routine from a weekend to a workweek. Or I ride Cosmo or Noah, our two five-gaited lesson horses.

Mondays are when I developed an ability to ride a slow gait and rack. Alyssa, after giving me all the instruction I needed, finally turned me loose on Cosmo in a barn we call the small arena and said, "Ride and figure it out."

I did. I felt quite accomplished—and thankful. Alyssa, in her own elegant, understated way, invited me to recognize that I could ride, and to step up into a level that helped horses as much as they helped me. She also always caught me up on the events of the barn: which babies were foaled and how they were doing; what horses are going to which show; and the humans that have as many quirks as horses.

"Horse barns are so much crazier than churches, I bet," she said once. I told her I doubted that because churches had all the idiosyncratic weirdness of humans mixed with Jesus, which was considerably more dramatic than humans and horses.

Because I usually have nowhere to go after I ride, Mondays are also days when I can watch the horses in the paddocks and visit the ones in the stalls. During foaling season, I meet the colts and fillies who have graced us with their new life. I watch them play in the paddocks and discover their legs as they gallop around. I watch them grow from gangly foals to yearlings, then fill out and up with muscle and become horses.

Watching horses in the fields and even in their stalls gives me parts of the story of who they are that go unseen by people who only come in, ride their horse, and leave. Those of us who take the time to stop and watch get to see how distinct their personalities truly are. Lilly, who is a delicate beautiful pony who trots around the ring with attitude to spare, is frightened of Styrofoam and George the Donkey. Yet in the field with the other lesson horses, she is large and in charge. Larry the palomino is her best friend, but he's not the king of the paddock.

I see the preferred playmates of different horses and the ones who prefer solitude. I've learned which horses will follow me out to the back gate for nuzzles and which ones stare at a distance with a suspicious side-eye as I walk to open the back gate. Some horses are talkers, who love to vocalize when they see a human they like or are ready to come in from their day in the paddock. Some horses are nappers. Nina is one of those; she loves to spend regular times of her day resting on the ground.

I've bathed horses, and I've learned who loves a bath to the point of ecstasy (CLo) and who has to be gently talked through the hose and sponge aspects of getting a bath. On lovely sunny days, I snap on the lead shank and let the newly bathed horses munch on grass while I simply stand and watch the sun glint off their wet coats and listen to the sounds of them breathe and eat.

Watching horses is a way of reading them, of letting the words of their movements, quirks, and vocalizations inform me of their wisdom and complexity. Watching horses sometimes invites me to engage with them. I scratch ears, nuzzle them and let them nuzzle me, and ride them enough to know their habits, likes, and dislikes.

Sabbath invites me simply to notice, to be, to give my time to allow these horses to tell me more of who they are. While their life isn't a secret life—it is there in the paddocks and the barns for all to see—remembering the Sabbath nudges me to stop and pay attention to this life that often goes unnoticed.

Horses are herd animals or band animals, meaning they live in small groups for safety and survival. Harem is my favorite word horse anthropologists use to describe the bands that horses live in, mainly in the wild. If you watch wild horses (or, more accurately, feral horses) in some of the many places they live in the world, they do live in harems—one stallion, a few mares, and usually some foals. Horses aren't particularly territorial. They roam, which likely plays a part in their evolutionary success. Horses can adapt to survive on all manner of forage. When territory is not the primary factor in the herd, harem, or band, relationships become essential to survival.

This interesting quirk of development, the horse's need of relationship, is likely one of the key factors in our horse-human relationship. Horses, because of their affinity for connections, seek out community, preferably with other horses, but humans will also do in a pinch.

Our horses at the barn don't live in harems, although I'm fairly sure Larry imagines he does, even though I think Lily is the only mare who likes him in the field. They have their own communities. The largest band lives in the outside paddock closest to the lesson barn. Larry and Lily are clearly a pair. Bucky, the little pony, plays by himself. Moe enjoys hanging out near the fence of the outside arena and bothering the other horses as they ride by in the outdoor riding arena. He likes to bother other horses in the paddock as well. Moose, a chestnut horse, loves to follow Luna, a paint mare, around. He clearly wants to be her friend. I'm not sure she's decided if she wants to reciprocate.

Then we have the indoor stalled horses. They get turned out each day to play in one of the fields. Nina and Darcy are the two older ladies who enjoy going out together. Nina does not like solitude. If she's turned out alone, she'll start to make noise after ten minutes or so. But with Darcy, they stay out for quite a while, enjoying their day in the field as two mature ladies who lunch together.

One evening in the barn, Julie and I were talking in the hallway, about five feet from Nina's stall. A few minutes into our conversation, Nina began to whinny and paw—not her usual behavior. Concerned that she was hurt or something was wrong, I went into her stall to see if she was okay. Julie followed me. We investigated her hooves, legs, and body. I looked for random things in the stall that would bother her. I checked her food bucket. Nina has a skill of pooing in her food bucket when she's annoyed by something, from construction in the barn to the layer of food that can harden and accumulate in the bottom of the bucket—Nina expects a clean plate for her grain.

But there were no strange things in her stall and no poo in her bucket. All was well.

So Julie and I continued our conversation in Nina's stall. After a few more moments, I realized Nina had maneuvered herself into our circle, pushing me to the side so she could stand among us. She was right there, a part of the discussion, listening, paying attention. Nina apparently likes to gossip as well as nap and eat peppermints.

Nina knows her community. She's a horse, and a horse's nature is to form bonds. Horses need community, much like humans.

A wonderful aspect of this inherent nature of horses to form bonds is to pay attention to cues. Horses listen, in a sense. They watch. They notice. They recognize and remember. All of these things, again, work together to create a bond with humans (because they need community) and an ability to read humans. This means horses learn in a fantastic way.

I've noticed that many of the horses at our barn behave differently with different riders. Some horses step up with certain riders, looking fancy and showy, in a way that simply can't be explained just because of a rider's ability. Some horses and riders simply don't get along. Larry is not a fan of male riders. I could argue that men might tend to ride with heavier hands than women, but I know many women riders who don't have soft hands and many men who do. Nina knows when a little person is on her, and trots and walks with a delicacy of a mother holding a newborn. Izzy had a clear preference for riders, a preference made known in the first trip around the arena. Horses will test riders to see what they can and can't get away with, and they learn quickly which riders will let the horse make the plan and which riders have other ideas.

Some riders come in, find their horse ready to ride, saddle up, and ride. When they are finished, they put the horse in a stall and leave. I'm sure, like so many of us, there are places to go and appointments to keep and tasks to do.

I've been there, rushed and pressured to meet deadlines and expectations.

But Sabbath reminds me of the value of presence over production, of the value of stopping to notice the world around me. My Sabbaths at the barn have taught me that time with horses is everything.

Some may consider Sabbath as a time of doing nothing. Perhaps that's true for them. But over the years, I'm astonished at the insight I've gained through my Sabbath times of "doing nothing" with horses. They have reminded me to value connections, relationships, and more subtle ways of knowing each other, by taking time to stop, to notice, to be in the present.

CHAPTER 15

The Holiness of Dirty Hooves

*R*iding horses is a dirty sport.

Not from a distance. From a distance, as you drive by one of the hundreds of scenic back roads in the Bluegrass region of Kentucky, the horses look sleek and impressive, and the paddocks where mares graze in the late spring are ripe with vivid green grass and awkward foals discovering their ability to trot and gallop.

Up close, however, those paddocks are as much mud as grass, and every equestrian worth her salt has a few stories of wading through mud to catch a horse during mud season, which runs from late fall until the ground freezes in late winter, then defrosts into mud again until the dryness of midsummer takes over, also known as fly season.

Going out into the field to catch a horse during mud season involves wearing muck boots, high plastic boots that will let you sink into a few inches or a few feet of slime. During mud season, I'm convinced that the mud will never dry and my memories of this as a green, lush field were a hallucination.

Step. Sink.

Balance.

Pull. Step. Sink.

Inevitably I have that one step where my leg and foot come out, but the boot doesn't. So there I stand, awkwardly balancing on one leg trying to get my foot back into the boot, not fall in mud, and work around the one horse who is fascinated by my human predicament and wants to help or see if I have treats.

I always have treats.

The horses I ride regularly know this, so they begin the game of nuzzle and nudge at my arms and my coat pockets as I untack them after our ride. They leave an artful ornamentation of slobber and drool on my clothes or my skin. Horses have amazingly sensitive mouths. Their upper lip is prehensile, which allows it to grasp blades of grass and pull them in. This prehensile lip also allows them to play with shirt sleeves, zippers, buttons, gloves resting on the ledge in their stall, or their grooming equipment. I also know horses who find joy in pulling brushes, curry combs, and hoof picks out of the grooming box when it's sitting on the floor of their stall as we groom them. Nina would be one of these.

Brushing horses during grooming, especially during shedding season, means you, too, will look like you've sprouted a winter coat. If I get really fortunate, the marriage of mud season and shedding season, usually in March, means I add all that shedded hair to the layer of mud on my jodhpurs from the walk to the barn or during the ride where their powerful gaits throw mud all over their belly and my jodhpurs. I'm sure all the patrons at my local grocery are excited when I stop by for milk and eggs sporting a layer of horse hair, equine slobber, and mud.

Before I rode horses, I never understood the value of mudrooms. Now I realize they are a necessity. They are the space I can pull off muddy boots and drop dirty riding pants, shaking off clumps of dirt and enough shavings and hay to fill a stall in my house.

Horse riding is a dirty business.

It is, however, the dirt that seems exceptionally holy to me. If not for the dirt that gets on horses, humans would miss the deeply connective act of grooming our horses. Grooming is calming, affectionate, appreciated, and messy for both horse and rider. Grooming is a behavior horses share with each other, and we share with them. In this liturgy of currying, brushing, combing, picking hooves, and washing, we bond with them in a way we simply can't do by riding them.

The day-to-day grooming involves me getting the horse, either from the field or from the stall, and haltering her. If it's been chilly, I pull off a horse-sized sheet or blanket, which can overtake me on some days with its size and weight. Then I search for the grooming tools I need. In the world of horse magazines, the grooming box is always placed in an elegantly styled cabinet, each item perfectly placed in the box. In a busy barn like Wingswept, grooming often involves a search in stalls for renegade brushes and hoof picks that didn't make it back into the grooming boxes, which are somewhere in the tack room, and rarely in the same place twice.

Brushes, curry combs, hoof picks, hoof grease, regular combs, and shedding blades are all pitched into the grooming box. They are well-used and often used, tossed into or near the box by riders getting horses ready or cooling them down, pulled out of the box by curious and playful horses, and gathered at the end of a riding day by whichever of us is last to put her horse up.

I dig around the box for a curry comb—an oval, flat comb with tiny little plastic teeth—and start at their necks, rubbing in circles to loosen dirt and hair. It's the equivalent of me using a loofah on my skin. Most horses love the minimassage and settle into the routine that will involve touch, rubs, and feel-good scratches. Then they get the first brush, a stiff brush that knocks off all the detritus the curry comb has loosened. My favorite brush isn't in the box, so I check the ledges of stalls.

Horse people are weird like this.

I find it, then get my preferred soft brushes while I'm on the prowl. Once I get my equipment, I start brushing. Outside horses, obviously, are dirtier and require a good going-over with a stiff brush to knock off caked-on mud, more than the horses that live in stalls.

As I brush, I chat with them, wondering what they've been into with all the mud, telling them about who will ride them this day. Today I'm helping Larry get ready. My friend Lettie owns him. Larry, like Nina, had a past show career. He was quite the successful young horse, but he's settled well into life as a lesson horse and the object of Lettie's love and affection.

"She's learning to canter," I remind Larry, who at times is finicky about picking up his canter, "So try not to be difficult today. You know how to canter." Larry doesn't care for his ears or his mouth to be touched, so I talk calmly as I brush off the mud that is decorating his forehead. For this task, I've switched to a smaller, softer brush, since his face and ear area need more detail work. Larry is a beautiful palomino . . . when he's clean. Since he lives outside in the fields, he's usually clean only before a show.

Competitive horse riding looks spotlessly clean, for horses and riders. When we show in the saddle seat discipline, we wear dress shirts, spotless riding pants, and vests, coats, and ties. Those replace the stained t-shirts and jodhpurs with holes worn in the heel area from years of riding and walking on jodhpurs that come down over our boots. Women's hair is pulled back into a neat, low bun. A jeweled tie bar keeps our collar and tie in place. Elegant black leather gloves replace the sweat-stained ones we work in day after day. When I am dressed to show, I could just as easily be an extra on *Downton Abbey*.

The horses are bathed and brushed to a spectacular shine. Their manes are combed. Their tails, things of wispy beauty that can be six feet long or more, are washed, conditioned, blown out, and brushed. Hollywood celebrities before a major award show don't have hair as coiffed as the tails of competitive Saddlebred horses before they take the show ring.

Horses know the difference between their day-to-day grooming and their show grooming, I think. If nothing else, the show grooming is a much more intense process. The everyday grooming is functional. We loosen dirt from their skin and coats and brush away the debris of their day. This ensures saddle pads, girths, and bridles don't rub and chafe, causing saddle sores or other irritations. As we groom, we also go over legs and backs and sides to see if there are any abrasions or bumps that need to be addressed.

Hooves are an area of particular concern. The saying "No hoof, no horse" is true. Hooves are the foundation of a horse. They aren't their feet, actually, but a single toe. Their hooves are made of keratin, the same stuff of our human fingernails. Unlike our fingernails, their hooves are filled with all manner of tiny bones and blood vessels. Their one toe, the hoof, supports their weight and provides the foundation for their movement.

The farrier at Wingswept takes amazing care of the horses' hooves, and our daily checking helps keep them sound. When

I groom, I check the hooves for cracks, for abscesses, for pieces of rock that are stuck uncomfortably in the edges.

Horse's hooves may be bare or shoed, depending on the horse and their hoof structure. Their hooves have divots and grooves that attract dirt, mud, pebbles, hay, and even poop. A fundamental part of getting the horse ready to ride and cleaning the horse after riding is picking the hooves.

I adore picking hooves—another weird horse people thing, perhaps. Picking out packed residue, brushing the edges of their horseshoes, and finally putting hoof grease on their hooves (it's like lotion for us) is the equivalent of saying, "Amen" after the prayer I offer at the end of a long day. I start with something messy, and carefully pull, pick, and brush until I'm looking at a clean hoof, ready for weight and movement.

Nina loves to be groomed, and she knows our routine so well she picks her hooves up for me in perfect order for me to clean them. I take the hoof pick and dig out all the mud, dirt, and mess she's accumulated in there, then tell her, "Good girl." She puts that hoof down and lifts up the next one.

Even with her cooperation, picking hooves is work. I have to bend down in a squat, and when I'm picking the hooves of certain horses, I'm wary of their propensity to bite or move suddenly. Some are less cooperative of shifting their weight from four to three legs, and need the added pressure of me leaning into their shoulders and legs to encourage them, a lean that I hope doesn't end with me splayed on the barn floor because I lost my balance. Some horses enjoy the game of challenging the person grooming them, just to see how difficult they can be about the whole affair. Some kick as well. While I find great satisfaction in digging the detritus out of horses' hooves, it's an act not without risk.

Cleaning feet played a deeply profound role in Jesus's ministry too. All four Gospels have an account of a woman anointing Jesus with ointment or perfume before his crucifixion. In two, Luke and John, she uses her hair to wash and dry his feet. This soft prayer is one of a grace and love that simply has no words.

And yet, the disciples have words. They criticize this display of love. This perfume is so costly. We could have sold it and used the money for the poor. Those criticizing these irrational acts of love often sound logical.

Jesus is having none of it. Leave her alone. Why are you bothering her?

They are bothering her, I suspect, because her lavish act of love bothered them. If I were at a dinner party with someone who preached words of love, words that scraped the layers of mud off souls caked with judgment and hate, and in response and thanks, a woman came in as we finished our meals and poured perfume over their feet while weeping and wiping feet with tears, I would be bothered.

Yes, the whole moment would be bothersome, but not simply because of the whole washing feet moment, but because we would be witnesses to grace, this unmerited, lavish expression of love. We might be forced to remember the messiness that has been splashed on us, coating us, soiling us, from our interactions with others.

We might realize we, too, are called to wash feet. Or pick hooves. And that we need our feet washed. We need to have the parts of us that ground us, that move us, and that support us on our journey, cleaned and cared for. Blisters need to be salved. Soreness needs to be massaged. Dirt needs to be washed.

We indeed are called to this, to express this lavish love to our fellow human beings who are, as Jesus says more than once during his earthy ministries, embodiments of him. "What you do to the least of these, you do to me." And we need to receive this lavish love and care.

When Jesus, on the night before he was crucified, washed his disciples' feet, they didn't understand the holiness of the act of the Messiah, kneeling down with a bowl of water and washing their feet, presumably dirty and dusty. Jesus even tells them, "You do not know now what I am doing, but later you will understand" (John 13:7).

All this washing of feet and picking of hooves are acts of profound gratitude and love. Yes, we're cleaning the dirt off, making something shiny and fresh. We're checking for places that need to be cared for and rested, and we're also acting in love, which is always somewhat risky. We can get bitten or kicked. We can fall backward into a pile of horse manure on the stall floor. We can have our expression of love rejected or mocked or judged.

Love is a dirty business. The love Jesus calls us to is messy and lavish. We are called to share it and receive it. It just so happens that washing the feet of horses, even with the risks, is safer for me than washing the feet of humans—perhaps because horses so freely receive this intimacy of relationship, even the ones who enjoy making it challenging with their quirks.

CHAPTER 16
The Color Purple

I think it pisses God off if you walk by the color purple in a field somewhere and don't notice it. . . . People think pleasing God is all God cares about. But any fool living in the world can see it always trying to please us back.
—Alice Walker, *The Color Purple*

One of my early memories is from nursery school in Greenville, Mississippi. I was four, sitting at the corner of a child-sized table, coloring a page from a coloring book. I can't remember the details of the picture drawn with heavy black lines, leaving open space for my chubby, preschool crayons to fill. I do remember there was a woman in the picture. Maybe it was playtime. Maybe we had color time. My four-year-old memory doesn't record those fragments.

What my memory did record is the purple crayon I held in my hand. I'd just finished coloring the woman's face purple and was intently working on adding this fabulous shade of God's imagination to her arms. The teacher stood over me and shared her disapproval for my color choice.

"Laurie," she said, with that same tone I have when I hear people don't use Duke's Mayonnaise in their deviled egg recipe, "you know better than to color a person's face purple."

No, actually, I didn't. I was four, and I loved the color purple. But because I was four, I thought this adult was correct, so I stopped coloring. I put down the purple crayon.

I didn't pick up a purple crayon to fill in the spaces that needed coloring in my soul for decades.

I wish I had been one of those children who didn't care what the teacher thought and continued to color everything purple. But I was a child, and as an adult, what I realize is I wish I had a nursery school teacher who realized four-year-olds and forty-year-olds could be creative in all sorts of ways that see beyond the hard facts of the reality of melanin and skin color.

I wish my soul had been formed in a family that invited and celebrated creativity, one that colored rampantly outside the lines. Instead, my family congratulated accolades that looked good on a resume, but never failed to add a cautionary statement of not resting on your laurels or how easily someone else could have accomplished the same thing.

I grew up a child in a family in a culture that didn't approve of coloring people's faces purple. So I didn't.

I found the path that was acceptable and appropriate, that excelled and exceeded in all the ways that looked admirable on a college application and a law school application and a life application. Valedictorian. College sorority president. College Hall of Fame. Law School.

On occasion, though, I would notice the color purple, its visual temptation of the world that existed not so much to accomplish, but to appreciate and realize. Most of the time this happened not because I chose to, but because God funneled me down a path that left few options.

A requirement for graduation from the University of Southern Mississippi when I attended was a physical education course, some number of hours doing something beyond sitting in a classroom and reading. My advisor noted in my junior year I needed to check this off the list rather than wait until the last minute. Of the classes that fit my overachieving schedule, Western horsemanship was the one that looked most interesting.

While I had ridden horses off and on, the off times far outweighed the on. My instructor fit the image of a Western cowgirl from a century ago. She was tall and rangy, with skin that had not seen sunscreen and hair in dire need of deep conditioning that she wore in a long center braid down her back. And of course she wore a straw cowboy hat with frayed edges.

I arrived at the university's horse barn, also in dire need of deep conditioning, with its mismatched wooden slats on the walls and gravel parking lot with more potholes than parking lot. I was ready to accomplish this class. My first riding instructor whose teaching approach was like a firm but humane chute to guide horses into a new corral, sat the entire class of five down at a picnic table to talk with us about the value of riding slowly.

I wondered if I should be taking notes, but no one else was, and this was a pass/fail class based on attendance (she'd already gone over that), so I figured I was okay.

Over thirty years her exact words have faded, but I remember her taking us into the barn and showing us all the equipment we'd be using—halters, bridles, girths, saddle pads, Western saddles, and grooming kits. And I remembered her holding out the grooming kits and saying this is how we began and ended our time with the horses, by grooming them slowly.

In my Western horsemanship class, my instructor, like my grandfather, believed that you couldn't call yourself a rider unless you got the horse ready, rode, and took care of the horse afterward. My grandfather never mentioned grace in that time, but in my now decade of faithful riding since then, I realize the time of grooming a horse is indeed a consecrated time of grace. When I am present to grace, I want the time to last, so I don't rush.

Savor it. Slowly.

My college-aged self, however, mostly saw this as a time that took more time than a class should. But, I reasoned, since I wasn't having to do any outside reading or take an exam, the drive to the barn, the two hours of preparation, riding, and then clean up, somehow worked out.

The me that rides a few times a week marvels at my younger self's ability to spend only two hours at the barn. One aspect of grace at the barn is the wonderful loss of time that occurs there. A quick trip to check on Nina or watch a friend ride her new horse mysteriously expands into the entire morning, an entire morning of being present.

But I was twenty and more concerned with being present to the list of accomplishments I was convinced that I needed to be worthy of a life worth living, so in the midst of my days of a double major, being involved in more extracurricular activities than there are football fans in the state of Alabama, and preparing to take the law school entrance exam, I went to the barn in the late afternoons once a week for riding lessons. My first job was to put a halter on Apple and crosstie her so I could groom her. Apple was a sweet Quarter Horse my instructor chose for me. She was my first experience with a beginner horse, the type who are steadfast and tolerant in ways that would qualify humans for sainthood. Apple was calm and kind, and she loved to be groomed.

Grooming isn't just a way to get dirt and sweat off of horses' coats so that the saddle pad and tack don't cause irritation. Grooming is an important way horses bond with those in their community. In the fields, horses will groom each other to keep flies and other annoying bugs off each other. A horse's physical stature doesn't allow for them to scratch their own mane and necks easily, so they have learned to allow other horses to move into their space. Horses use their lips and teeth to rub, nip, and scratch each other's necks and withers in the intimate and necessary act of grooming.

Horses are fans of space. When we ride, we ideally keep one horse length between horses to avoid pinned ears or a lifted leg that signals a space violation and potential kick. Grooming, however, can't be done at a distance, so to groom and be groomed, horses must relax their natural boundary, with horses and humans, and let us come closer than their natural tendencies would normally allow. Grooming for horses is not just a practical way to scratch itchy places and remove bugs, it also is a physical expression of bonding.

Grooming lowers a horse's heart rate when they are brushed, rubbed, and nuzzled on their necks. It feels good physically and emotionally for horses.

It has the same effect on me. When I brush Nina, I breathe in her scent, that intoxicating incense of hay, sweet feed, sweat, and grace that is Nina. Every horse has its own smell that those of us who stop long enough and breathe deeply enough know as we are getting them ready to ride or grooming them after we've ridden.

As I brush Nina, I rest my head on her shoulder and feel the steady, strong beat of her heart, some seven to nine times the size of mine. Hers is big enough to pump blood through her elegantly large body and hold space for my heart too. Our grooming time almost always culminates with Nina leaning her head into my hand, letting me know how much she loves when I scratch the place at the base of her ears, so please keep doing that. She drops her head to breathe on the back of my neck. It's an act of mutual trust and intimacy, and for a few moments, we groom each other in the intimate act eons of nature developed that will almost always leave a fair amount of Nina slobber on me.

But over thirty years ago, I groomed Apple because it was third on the list. Our instructor had a list written on the chalkboard in the barn to help us remember.

1. Halter and tie horse
2. Get groom box
3. Groom horse

My overachieving, goal-oriented, who-has-time-to-notice-the-color-purple self loved lists. Lists gave me a sense of accomplishment, seeing all the things I needed to do and checking them off when done. Lists were a tidy framework of the rules I'd created. Do these things, and all shall be well, and you won't get scolded for coloring a human face purple.

Being in the barn was very outside my comfort zone. I thought I knew the rules, but I wasn't sure. Apple was a horse, and while I could learn some basic guides, a relationship with this equine was quite different from my relationships with college friends.

In this experience in the barn that felt outside my comfort zone, I appreciated the list as I groomed Apple. Curry comb. Hoof pick. Brush. Then I saddled Apple and had my lesson. Then all the grooming again, just in reverse.

Apple's stall, like all the stalls in the barn, faced an open walkway that looked out westward into the piney woods of southern Mississippi. Our lessons ended after five. And slowly, over the semester, as I would groom Apple after our lessons, I had glimpses of being present to a moment without needing to put it on the applications of my life. Unfortunately, most graduate schools and subsequent potential legal employers (and for that matter, seminaries) don't think learning to sit a trot or untangle a mane are quite the achievements of being invited to be a member of the school's highest honor society.

As I groomed Apple and listened to my cowgirl instructor talk about the value of slowness in riding, I occasionally would notice the sun set over the rails of the stalls. Light would ease down the wall of Apple's stall as I circled the curry comb on her dun coat, releasing the dust and dirt. Then I found the stiff brush, laying the bristles against her coat and rolling them as I brushed her so that the tips of the bristles wouldn't stick her skin. I leaned into her front right shoulder as I ran my hand down the length of Apple's leg, urging her to pick up her hoof. With the hoof pick, I cleaned her wide hooves. Then I repeated the move three more times.

I finished our time with the soft brush. Apple loved to have her face brushed, and as I worked, she breathed deeply. Her eyelids closed. In this space, with Apple, achievement didn't matter. Accomplishment didn't matter. Apple mattered, and my presence with her mattered. At the end of our time together, the sun was beginning to set.

Sunsets in Mississippi, sunsets everywhere, from my experience, let the sun drown in the rich colors of creation: deep roses, murky yellows, and outrageous purples. And in those moments, with Apple in the midst of her stall, I noticed the color purple. I noticed the power of slowing down enough to feel the heartbeat of another creature of God. I felt the loose hair from Apple on my skin, stuck there by the ever-present Mississippi humidity.

I noticed the beauty that was around me, in the present. Not what I needed to accomplish or how I'd not gotten something done this day and surely it would be a mark on my permanent record. I found joy in horses, who weren't purple, but who were beautiful and bigger than me in many ways and who made me stop and notice.

My twenty-year-old self didn't find the purple crayon and hold onto it in that moment, but maybe a part of me held on to this gift of presence, of noticing, and of slowness that was within my reach. I had held it, in the brushes and in Apple's tack and in the evenings we rode.

Noticing the glory of God, the moments that shift and shake me out of lists and accomplishments, is a slow process. Another almost two decades would pass before I noticed the color purple and let it reside in my soul.

Then, a few years ago, as I was repainting the rooms of my home, I was choosing a color for what I call my room, the space where I pray and write and read and be. I picked out a deep shade of purple, one of the shades in sunsets.

"Not too many people paint a room purple," the clerk at the paint store said.

"I do," I replied. "Finally."

CHAPTER 17

Margaritas, Mares, and Ministry

━━━━◈◈◈━━━━

*A*dult camp requires a good sense of humor, a healthy supply of Advil, and Mexican food and margaritas at the restaurant down the road from the barn. Summer riding camps for youth are not a new thing. It's summer. Kids love horses, and a week at the barn riding multiple times a day, learning about horses, and playing is a perfect option.

But why should the kids have all the fun? After complaining and lobbying for a couple of years to Stephanie that we also wanted to have some summer fun at the barn complete with horses and crafts, we finally got an adult riding camp on the calendar. One week in July of riding several times a day, learning about horses and the value of sunscreen and Advil, and crafts.

We even had a few field trips to an equine rehabilitation center and a world-renown equine vet. Several of us noted that with all the money we'd sent through the years to the world-renowned equine vet, they should have given us free t-shirts to go with our tour. We each got a magnet.

Our days ended with late-afternoon chips, salsa, sodas, and margaritas.

Margaritas and mares have one thing in common. Well, maybe two. I love them both, and they are both salty. An old horse truism is, ask a stallion, tell a gelding, and negotiate with a mare. Author Janet Morris wrote, "Nothing walks the earth more savage than a mare enraged." I know riders who will not own a mare because of their reputation as salty and difficult, not entirely an undeserved reputation.

Mares are not the members of the horse world that stand in the corners and watch the world go by. In the wild, they have their own hierarchy in bands, and a mare will refuse a stallion she does not want. Mares frequently run the show, in both wild bands and in paddocks. Watching mares at Wingswept, I've seen a fascinating range of behavior to get what they want, from the out-and-out fierceness of a well-placed kick to move a nosey gelding away from their space to the calculated patience of knowing just when we leave a certain gate open at the same time each day, allowing for them to sneak in and munch on grain.

Stallions provide impressive shows when they are establishing dominance or trying to mate. They rear up, blow, and stomp. Mares, however, are distinctly more subtle about their behavior, but no less impressive. I suspect that mares, who are generally smaller than stallions and lack a dominant physical size, learned over the eons how to find their own path to surviving and even thriving by using their wiles instead of their weight. Perhaps this is my own projection, but I've found mares more attune to the emotional intricacies and physical skills of the rider, and then take advantage of them when doing so suits them.

Amazing Amy was certainly living up to her full-on mare reputation today, mostly because she'd quickly realized I was not confident about riding her. Amy was in training as a show horse, but because she was not going to be competitive at the level for which her owner had hoped, the owner decided to see how Amy would be as a lesson horse for intermediate and advanced riders.

Amy is a stunning bay mare with a neck arch and a high step that makes for exquisite photos and a deft lesson for riders. She's acutely smart and supremely confident in herself, and she makes you work for your ride. She's also salty. I've watched a few riders get shifted from the saddle on her back to the ground when she expressed her displeasure about something they were doing or just decided she'd had enough. She full-on rodeoed with me one day, and I managed to get her stopped and walking before my instructor Alyssa got on her to adjust Amy's attitude a bit.

I finished that ride on another horse and hoped I wouldn't have to ride Amy again. That hope ended on Wednesday of adult camp.

This Wednesday afternoon of adult camp, we had a guest instructor. She was working with us on equitation, a focus on the rider and how well she exhibits the abilities and skills of her horse while maintaining the standards of saddle seat equitation. Saddle seat equitation notices where the rider is sitting so that the horse has the best center of balance. This allows the natural front leg action to be more animated with a high trot. Equitation also notices where our hands are—is there a straight line from horse's mouth to rider's elbow? Is our upper body straight with shoulders back while looking relaxed, rather than stiff or poised? And is there a straight line from shoulder, hip, heel with toes just under the knees?

Oh, and all this should be done elegantly with little unintended motion at every gait.

I am not an equitation rider. Like many sports, there is a body type that simply looks better in equitation competition, and it's not mine. That does not mean, however, that I get to dismiss the value of taking care of my body position while I ride. Nancy, our guest instructor for the afternoon, shared that good, solid form in equitation allowed the horse to be her best. If we as riders are leaning forward, holding our hands too high so that we pull on their mouths, or any number of things humans do when we ride slack and lazy, we give unclear signals to the horse about riding. This almost always results in an unpleasant ride.

Or, in the case of Amy, screwing the cap off the saltshaker and dumping it all over me with her excessive saltiness.

She was not the mare I really wanted to ride for this lesson. I wanted to be confident and show Nancy I could ride a horse. Amy liked to remind me I had much to learn. But here I was, riding Amy.

Nancy had us all enter the ring at a walk, then pick up our trot. After a few rounds around the arena, she pulled us into the middle and talked. She asked us what our biggest obstacle to riding was.

The first group that had gone all had really professional rider sounding answers. They were working on not rocking in the canter or having softer hands. I didn't think any of those things. My biggest obstacle was confidence. But from what all the first group riders had said, I began frantically thinking of a more impressive sounding answer as I sat on the fence watching them do some final passes around the arena.

I was still thinking about my response, dancing between my tendency to lean forward in the saddle when I got nervous or keeping my shoulders back when I took a corner. Those sounded like I'd been riding a while and had some of the basics down, but still recognized I needed improvement. Nancy asked the most experienced rider among us, who had been riding since she was a young girl, to go first.

"Confidence," she said, with her voice cracking a bit.

I, along with every other rider in the group (there were four of us), nodded. We all went around the circle, and said the same thing. I was both astonished and relieved. The four of us were very different riders. Two had been riding for decades. Julie and I started about the same time. All of us showed horses. If you'd asked me prior to the circle of unconfident riders, I would not have suspected any of the other three riders struggled with confidence.

But here we were, with our varying degrees of time in the saddle and abilities, all admitting we lacked confidence. Nancy smiled, then began to share with each of us what she noticed and something to try to find ourselves as confident riders.

She came to me.

"What do you do when you preach?" she asked.

What does this have to do with the price of bourbon in Kentucky, I wondered, but I thought about all the small things that happen when I preach, even before I preach. I spend hours, even days, reading the Scripture on which I'm going to preach. I pray as I read, asking God to work with me, guide and push me to find the words the congregation needs to hear. I feel the congregation as I preach, the energy of the room.

"Preaching takes confidence," Nancy continued, sharing how getting up in front of people Sunday after Sunday talking about the hard things in life was something I did confidently, or at least mostly confidently. "Preaching takes cooperation," she said.

"You're trying to control Amy, not cooperate with her. Sit in the saddle and ride like you're preaching. Preach to Amy. She'll listen."

Preaching and teaching is an act of cooperation and of relationship between the speaker and those who listen. Even though usually one person is speaking, I am not speaking to a wall. Those who listen are participating with their presence, even their prayers. While some may think preaching is limited to something clergy do on holy days with a congregation listening, Nancy reminded me it is also a form of communication that we all embody when we share about our relationship with God with an appropriate vulnerability.

Nancy also reminded me about the shadow side of preaching, which was what I was doing to Amy—using my presence to control Amy in a pompous and self-righteous way. Amy was having none of this type of preaching.

A quote attributed to St. Francis of Assisi is to preach the gospel at all times and, if necessary, use words. No evidence exists to suggest he actually said this, but the quote reminds me that preaching isn't about exhortation or control. Preaching isn't even something only clergy do. Preaching is a relationship that honors, respects, and loves the other.

Amy didn't need for me to share the history of Paul's letter to the Romans or what forgiveness looks like in real life. But I did know the feeling in my soul of knowing God was with me as I shared the gospel in the many ways we are all called to preach the gospel in our lives. I knew how I felt cared for and seen when someone preached the gospel to me with a hug, a nod of affirmation, even by handing me a tissue when I needed to wipe away tears. That was the sermon I needed to preach to Amy, one that was filled with cooperation and respect for both of us.

So, for the first time, I didn't tentatively ask Amy to trot. I sat in the saddle, stretched up in the same way I center myself in the pulpit, and said, "Trot," with the same tone I invite God to get between my words and the souls of those listening to my sermon, that we will all be moved to love.

"Look at that," Nancy commented.

I could feel the difference. Amy was still a salty, sassy mare with all sorts of energy and assurance. She still loved to challenge her riders. But for the first time in riding her, I felt a partnership, a collaboration, instead of me desperately trying to hang on. I rode with her. She, being a mare, also deemed me worthy enough to ride with me. I preached to Amy, and she preached to me.

CHAPTER 18

Wednesday Night Riding Club

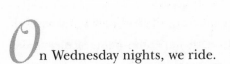

*O*n Wednesday nights, we ride.

I'm not sure when Wednesday nights became the adult riding night. Like many holy things, our group came into being slowly and somewhat naturally, until it seemed like Wednesday night rides had existed forever and we couldn't imagine our lives without it. We rode on Wednesday nights because we as adults worked, and 5:30 p.m. was the time we could get there. I think Anita and Stuart, a wife and husband who ride, were the initial, unintentional founders, and then gradually through the months and years, other adults joined.

I'd heard about the Wednesday night rides with some envy but was unable to come. St. Michael's had a Wednesday evening Eucharist, as many churches do. So each Wednesday, they rode, and I prayed in church.

Life moves, as it does, and the initial Wednesday night group of those worshiping regularly moved away or died. We missed them as we continued to gather and pray. Others came in the spring and summer, but not in the late fall and winter because they didn't drive in the dark. Then, with only a few of us, we wondered if the Wednesday evening service had lived its life, and perhaps should be paused for the summer just to see.

So, for the first time in over five years, I had Wednesday nights open.

"Come ride," Stephanie said one Thursday evening, when I rode, suggesting I could join the Wednesday night group.

"But those are the good riders," I replied, a bit nervous to ride with the grown-ups. I didn't consider myself a grown-up rider. I considered myself an adult who was barely competent on a horse. Stephanie rolled her eyes in that way that told me I was now riding on Wednesdays for the summer.

I felt all my nerves in the pit of my stomach as I drove out to the barn my first night. And my second. And my fiftieth. Anita is a true cowgirl. Several of the riders had ridden longer than I'd been alive. I knew I was swimming in the deep end. I told myself I wasn't alone, that others had joined in the past months who didn't have decades of riding experience.

This logic didn't truly comfort me. I was still quite sure I was over my head.

We did patterns, sequences of gaits and movements to sharpen our ability to communicate clearly to our horses and think ahead. We worked on lead changes with our canters. We rode different horses and had our favorites. We rode the ones that elicited deep sighs of resignation and some apprehension as we prepared to get in the saddle. With this group, I grew up as a rider.

Ride with better riders, I realized, and I got better.

"I miss praying in the church on Wednesday nights," one parishioner told me after a Sunday service.

I wanted to agree with her, but my soul found praying on Wednesday nights at the barn more edifying and more honest for me. Too often on Wednesday nights when I led the Eucharist, I felt the expectations of being the priest magnified.

I was supposed to say something insightful and meaningful. I was supposed to notice the unspoken needs of those who sat in the pews and ask them about these needs. I was supposed to be something I couldn't always be. The yoke of those expectations, both the ones I wrapped around my own shoulders and the ones dropped on me by others, stifled my prayers.

Not so at the barn, in the arena. Riding with the adults, I prayed honestly, with raw humility. My prayers were often along the lines of, "Please I hope I don't fall off tonight," or "Lord, I just can't ride Izzy," or, "Jesus, just let my stomach stop aching from nerves."

My prayers were answered by horses, who challenged and comforted me. Izzy and Amy made sure my humility as a rider never faded. CLo and Larry taught me that I could, indeed, step up a horse to another level because I as a rider could step up. Nina reminded me I always knew where home was on her, whenever I felt like I was swimming too deep for too long. She was always there to let me ride for a respite.

My prayers were answered by humans too. Different adults came and went. Some stopped in for a while, visiting Kentucky for a month or so and riding with us. Some came to try out this thing called riding. But our group, our firmly fixed and steadfast barn family, came week after week. We saddled up and rode.

We ride to encourage each other, challenge each other, and laugh with each other, as those in a deep relationship do. We carry on conversations in the arena, asking questions on one lap, then waiting until we come back around and pass each other to answer.

Stephanie will call us into a two-point position, when we stand in the stirrups as the horses we're riding trot around the arena, our backsides out of the saddle. Two-point is a position that strengthens legs and core muscles and improves our balance. Somewhere over the Wednesdays Stuart made the rule that he only two-points one lap around the arena. I like to see how long I can hold it until my calves start to burn. Stuart accuses me of showing off. I probably am. But I've also developed really solid calf and quad muscles.

When we canter, Steph isn't satisfied with us cantering our horses with a basic level of skill. Anyone can do that, I imagine her thinking. So she's invented games. The cantering game means we can't have our horse fall out of the canter or pass another horse while we canter. We get competitive. Over the years of playing, we've developed strategies. We laugh. And our riding has improved.

Stephanie challenges us with other games and drills. She's often shocked by our inability to follow simple directions. The cone drill is particularly mind-blowing for us, with all our advanced degrees and life experiences. Stephanie puts out sets of cones in varied colors, then we have to trot through them in the order of colors she calls out.

"Red, blue, green, and yellow," she says.

I promptly go through the orange ones, then the yellow ones. Julie, who came a few years ago when her instructor retired, goes through the blue ones first.

"Really?" Stephanie asks.

"We're old!" we say.

"You're riders," Stephanie replies and makes us do the cone drill again.

We laugh at our limitations, at not knowing how to follow directions. And we feel the joy of play. Adults too often forget we need to play. Horses play, chasing each other around the field and nudging at things they discover. On Wednesday nights, the horses and our instructor remind us to play.

We work on the basics. Are our toes facing forward? Are we keeping our knees rolled in and our lower legs still when we post? Steph reminds us to keep our shoulders back and sit deeply and quietly in the saddle at the canter.

She also notices things like our thumbs. "Turn them up," she says as I ride by.

"How do you notice my thumbs?" I ask.

"It's Steph. She notices everything," Julie replies, passing me on Fatimo.

I wonder what my thumbs have to do with good riding, but I know they do. So I pay attention to my thumbs.

After we ride, we bring our horses into the barn and untack them. We take off bridles and saddles and put on halters. We brush the horses and rub them down and talk to the horses and to each other. We talk about the work that we're doing that feels exciting or exhausting. We share our frustrations about horses and ourselves. We often talk about our frustrations about horses because we can't talk clearly about the frustrations of our own lives. We've learned that shorthand.

Sometimes I am silent when the world feels too much and if I do anything but brush my horse, I will burst into tears. And on Wednesday nights, my barn family honors my silence. But by Thursday, I'll get a text. "Just checking on you."

On Wednesday nights, we remind each other that yes, we can ride. We can also play and pray, in the way horses and friends allow both to happen with honesty and love. A reality for many of us is that our riding is the thing that keeps us grounded. The trauma of life shakes us, shakes me, blows me sideways, and twists me in the gales of the distress of not being able to help.

On those nights, when I come to the barn shaken and stirred, I sometimes have good rides. But I also sometimes don't. I've had plenty of those rides. When I do, I want to believe I can't ride.

Those Wednesday night riders tell me otherwise.

When they tell me I can ride, to have confidence, I remember I can have shaky rides that don't feel solid, but that doesn't mean I'm not a rider. I can have days and weeks when I feel shaky about my faith, about all that is love and forgiveness, but that doesn't mean I'm not a child of God.

We've talked about the difference between styles of jodhpurs and the grief of losing dear friends. We've wiped down horses with towels, rubbing them as they dry, then passed the towels to another to wipe tears, if needed, on exceptionally shaky weeks. We sweep the barn floor of renegade shavings and hay and find solace in an act that is complete with a clean floor, a respite from our careers as lawyers, clergy, medical professionals—lives that have few moments of completeness.

Somewhere in our moments, we discovered the power of the phrase, "You've got this." Its origins are vague and unknown at Wingswept, but it became the final affirmation before we ride into the show ring. Amid all the excitement and the nerves and the wobbly confidence that is riding into an arena to be judged on your ability to ride a horse and let the horse be fabulous, one of us says, "You've got this."

In the chaos and joy of life, in the times when I want to scream until the heavens fall, and in the times when I doubt my ability to post a trot or to help hold the grief of someone who has experienced a deep loss, I go out on Wednesdays and ride. In our rides, in our relationships, in our deep community with each other and the horses, we tell each other in so many ways, "You've got this."

PART FOUR

IN THE PRESENCE OF GOD, GRACE, AND HORSES

*C*hristianity is an impressive blend of influences and flavors. We forget that in the years and decades immediately following the crucifixion and resurrection of Jesus Christ, there were no neatly bound Bibles telling the story of humanity's encounters with God or catechisms to summarize religious beliefs in a tidy question and answer format.

Christians were a ragtag confederation of believers, and a cursory reading of early Christian hymns, writings, and liturgies reveal that their beliefs were varied and diverse. There was certainly a Jewish influence. We do well not to forget that Jesus himself, as well as the vast majority of his first disciples, were Jews.

We also find the Hellenic influence, the Greek ways of thinking, in the developing Christian church. The writings of early church fathers like Clement of Alexandria and Ambrose of Milan reflect the influence of Platonism and other Greek schools of philosophy. Where that shows up is in the Christian comfort with logic, that we can explain all things God and our beliefs, and such desire for explanations and clarifications is a good and holy thing.

We really like definitions. My own Episcopal Church, like many churches with a value of the logical and intellectual, has a catechism that explains things, as much as God can be explained.

In the catechism of the Episcopal Church, a boldface-typed question asks, "What is grace?"

The answer is a packed sentence: "Grace is God's favor towards us, unearned and undeserved; by grace God forgives our sins, enlightens our minds, stirs our hearts, and strengthens our wills."[8]

The sentence is a collection of ancient bones, held together with words from theological tomes by patriarchs and matriarchs of the church, prayers from the mystics, and hymns from the artists. Bones are foundational. Bones give us structure and form so we aren't a blob of substance oozing everywhere, unable to stand and move.

Bones, though, only get us so far with God. God is embodied. The teachings and experiences of God are best shared through the stories of God and humans—our love, our hate, our absurdities, and our responses to grace.

Grace meets us every day. Its presence in the mundane and smallness of my days and weeks astonishes me, when I remember to pay attention. God's grace is present in the times I lay my head on Nina's side and hear her heart beat. After a few moments, our breaths will synchronize and our spirits are simply present to each other as we stand in her stall, surrounded by hay and an occasional barn cat.

And when I am at the barn, shaky and wobbly and a bit broken from the reality of life that often is lacking grace, I find grace embodied in horses. Horses invite me to listen more deeply, with more than just my ears. They give me a new way to know I am heard.

On particularly hard days when my soul feels a bit raw around the edges and I can't hear myself that well, I go into Nina's stall and lay my head on her shoulder. She nuzzles me and stands, listening to me need reassurance. I listen to her heart. She feels mine.

In God's grace, we hear each other.

CHAPTER 19
My Soul Yearns

As the deer longs for the water-brooks,
so longs my soul for you, O God.
My soul is athirst for God, athirst for the living God;
when shall I come to appear before the presence of God?
—PSALM 42:1 (*Book of Common Prayer*)

*A*fter six weeks of not riding, I climbed in the saddle—
my saddle. It was polished and clean. It rested on Spencer. As
I eased into it, I wondered what finally riding after six weeks
of not riding would feel like to both of us.

I started to think about how to hold my reins. Most
Saddlebreds ride with two reins, a snaffle rein and a curb
rein. If you asked me to explain how you hold them, I would
have difficulty. I told my brain to quit trying to explain and
simply pick them up. My fingers knew where to go, exactly
how to weave the strips of leather between my fingers to hold
the snaffle rein and the curb rein. My legs knew how to drop
long and out. My knees knew how to roll in and fix my thigh
into the correct angle. I let stillness and joy overcome me as
Spencer walked around the arena.

Six weeks before this moment, I texted Stephanie, my
riding instructor. "I'm at the barn. I'm going to ride, but I'm
on a conference call."

I had driven out early for my usual Wednesday night ride on a generously warm mid-March day. March in Kentucky can be viciously cold with teases of spring. This day was one of the latter, so the group of adults who ride on Wednesday evenings would be outside tonight. This group, all of whom have ridden for years, many of us with each other for years, is my support group. They are, indeed, my people.

So, after the last few days, I needed to ride horses with my people tonight—because the last few days had been something out of the first thirty minutes of a new dystopian series on Netflix.

I'd been listening to the reports of COVID-19 that started weaving into the news in January. I'd flown to a retreat in Monterey, California, at the end of January. On my flight back, I noticed a larger than usual number of people wearing masks in the airport. I'd spent a week with clergy colleagues to pray, reflect, and plan the coming year.

And oh, did I have plans.

All of which were looking shaky with the conference call I was on with our diocesan bishop, in consultation with health professionals and the governor of Kentucky, who was considering suspending in-person worship because of what was quickly being recognized as a global crisis. We as a church did not have a missional strategy, playbook, or strategic plan for this.

What I did know is I had gone to lunch on Tuesday with two good friends, and today I was sitting in my Subaru underneath an oak tree with the beginning of new leaves just peeking out on the branches while I was on a conference call.

Last Sunday had been different—lots of sanitizer and telling parishioners to pass the peace at a distance. Also, taking communion only in the host was fine. Math in the church is creative. Jesus is fully present in the bread and the wine, or the bread only, or the wine only. That was a few days ago, I reminded myself, even though the time between last Sunday and this late Wednesday afternoon felt like several months ago.

"But it's important to remember there are only five confirmed COVID cases in Kentucky right now," one priest said, pulling me back into the moment, the weird, dystopian moment that marked the beginning of church in the time of COVID-19.

Silence met his observation. I wanted to agree, wanted to believe the worst estimates of half a million Americans dead was an absurd number, and that our discussions to pause in-person worship would be for a few Sundays and life would return to normal. Easter this year will be amazing, I thought.

Stephanie texted back as another clergyperson droned on: "You're riding Maria. It's her first time outside since last fall. Good luck."

Maria is a beautiful mare who has taught me much about riding with her ability to be fancy and particular about how she cares to be ridden. Maria expects her riders to ride her, not simply to sit in the saddle. Yet she also doesn't want her riders to override her, to fidget and move unnecessarily. She expects balance.

She also reserves the right to be silly at times, to jump from a corner or some other action she deems worthy of her energy. She's my go-to girl for horse shows. As I'm getting ready to show, I have all the nerves of showing swirling in my stomach. I fuss with my shirt, making sure it's tucked in. I check and recheck my boots and underpasses, the elastic strips that run under my boot sole to keep my jodhpurs from riding up as I ride. I ask myself why I put myself through this, this nervous energy of showing.

Then I settle in the saddle on Maria's back and hold the reins. I cluck her forward into the warm-up ring, and with her first steps, she shakes my nerves from my body and reminds me simply to ride. After one particularly heavy week in ministry, I almost scratched from a show that was coming up that weekend. Anita reminded me of that feeling of riding into the show ring and feeling the wind on my face as Maria trotted like the champion she is down the first rail.

"The world falls away. It's just you and Maria," she said.

Yes. The world does fall away when I ride her.

I adore her for this reason. Given that this was her first time in the outside arena, I fully expected Maria to have many high energy moments. Tonight, I needed to ride Maria. I needed good luck, not only in my ride on her, but in what was to come. And I needed the world to fall away as the March breeze blew in my face as I rode her.

> As the deer longs for the water-brooks, so longs my soul for you, O God. My soul is athirst for God, athirst for the living God; when shall I come to appear before the presence of God?

For almost a decade, no matter the stress, grief, or joy of ministry, I found time on horseback to help me center, to help me find silence and space to let feelings swirl and be, suddenly to find an ending to the sermon, or simply to remember who I am outside all the roles and expectations of my life. Horses and the people associated with them give me perspective and give me a reality check. A ride on a horse opens my eyes to my emotional energy, especially when I've fallen into the delusion of telling myself I'm calm, fine, or okay when I'm not. A shifting, unsettled horse more often than not reminds me to take some breaths. The horse, after all, depends on me to get myself centered to have the ride we need to have.

I managed two more rides in the next week. The entire country was rushing to buy toilet paper, but I was rushing to ride horses. Then I got the text all of us at the barn knew was coming but didn't want to admit.

"The barn is closed because of COVID-19 until further notice."

The church was closed, as well, to in-person worship until further notice. The world as we knew it was closed until further notice.

I was too stunned to weep at this immediate and consequential loss. I, a master of catastrophizing, couldn't even begin to weep at the losses I could imagine would be coming.

I did overfunction, doing everything and anything that I could do, at least at the church. I began doing the weekly e-newsletters and updating the website and planning the liturgies and searching online for bleach. When I sat down long enough, I asked my assisting priests about online worship. I talked to lay leaders about the church budget and began to get honest about positions that couldn't continue if this lockdown went on for months. I'd received a phone call from a parishioner who was in the hospital and scared. Pandemic protocols, all needed and reasonable, meant that they were alone.

"I wish you could come see me."

"I wish I could come see you," I replied.

I prayed with her on the phone, a fine prayer in God's sense of prayer. But it felt like a poor substitute to sitting next to a wonderful, fearful person and holding their hands while we ventured through the valley of the shadow of death.

I sat out in my garden and cried, then noticed how dirty the church windows were on this side of the building where the mud splashed up when the rain hit the dirt with force. I took a bucket of soapy water and washed the windows.

"Sounds like overfunctioning to me," my priest friend Peter said when I talked to him that night.

"It is, but I can't ride, which is what I usually do when I feel helpless and overwhelmed."

"Come do my windows next time."

We laughed, because both of us were tired of crying.

I couldn't ride, but I could talk to my barn family. Steph and Alyssa shared pictures and videos of the horses we loved. Nina, who had never been much of an outside horse, was loving her nights in the fields with her horse friends.

"Is this Nina?" I texted back in response to a picture of her grazing way out in the paddock with Izzy and Maria near her.

"Yep. She's enjoying life."

At least there was that, I thought. I also prayed, and prayed, during six weeks of wandering in the desert without a horse. I felt longing, yearning, and aching for that holy presence that had become such a part of my life. Having it suddenly gone felt like part of my ability to breathe had been stifled.

As the deer longs for the water-brooks, so longs my soul for you,
O God. My soul is athirst for God, athirst for the living God;
when shall I come to appear before the presence of God?

The mystics of the church are our master class guides on longing. They write voraciously of longing for God, for communion and unity with Jesus, all while knowing it will never fully come on this side of the kingdom of heaven.

Christian mysticism and those who practice it, called mystics, are broadly defined as those who yearn for and engage in an inner experience of God, rather than strictly adhering to an intellectual one. Their experience of God does not exclude intellect, but recognizes that God cannot be reduced to the rational explanations. Mystics yearn for a unitive experience, which is a constant task of contemplative prayer. It's a life of praying without ceasing.

Their yearning is akin to me reaching for the horse blanket that's been put on the top shelf in the tack room that's just out of my reach. I stretch and stand on my tiptoes, and I can just touch it, but I can't get a grasp on it.

The mystics would stay in that place of stretching and reaching and being.

I eventually go get a step stool.

Which is to say we can all have mystical moments with God, but some are called to a particular life of constant contemplative prayer while others find different ways. Mystics see value in yearning, in the constant awareness of our incompleteness and craving for the something more that can only be found in God. From the very beginnings of our human encounters with God, mystics have made their presence known in faith, mostly by finding space to contemplate God that was away from familiar surroundings. Desert Mothers and Fathers went into the wilderness around Egypt and lived in caves, away from the noise of cities and church politics of the day. Anchoresses walled themselves into small cells adjoined to churches to attain divine solitude. Even Thomas Merton found his own place alone with God, away from the day-to-day life of his cloistered monastic life into a hermitage, an even more private retreat.

Mystics remind us that sometimes we need to stop letting all the noise from the world take up space in our lives. We need simply to be alone with God. Human souls yearn, and yet we often fill them with noise, busyness, and activity so we don't have to be present with the very real and holy experience of incompleteness, the deep need for something more. I'd kept myself spectacularly busy with writing COVID-19 protocols, working on digital worship, and washing church windows.

I did not want to be in a cell alone with God. I had no interest in sitting in a desert cave to pray without ceasing, and Merton's monastery and hermitage were closed to visitors because of the pandemic. Yet, I found myself scattered and smothered under the weight of the nothingness that I could touch and push against.

I yearned, deeply and painfully, and for the first time in almost a decade, discovered the deep yearning I had for my relationship with God through horses. I sat with the absence of horses in my life. I felt the loss of the way I touched God when I touched their bodies and felt the warmth of life under their profoundly sensitive horse skin. I found the hole where only the prayers I could pray on horseback were uttered.

"Naughting" is the term mystics use to speak of being present with the absence of God. It reminds us that God does not abandons us, but that we in our journey of faith will have profound moments where we can palpably feel a yearning and desire to seek God and a deeper knowledge of God or simply an absence of God's presence. Julian of Norwich, an English mystic, in her *Revelations of Divine Love*, spoke of seeking God, recognizing she "lacked him; and this is and should be our ordinary undertaking of this life."[9]

Common parlance says absence makes the heart grow fonder.

Absence can help us clear out the things we've been holding on to for reasons of habit, routine, and assorted other ideas that seem good at the time. Absence can also help us discover what we don't yearn for, especially over the course of almost two months.

In the absence of routine, I had time to feel the space left by not being able to go to the barn. I loved sitting each morning in quiet prayer with God, and I felt the loss of the incarnational prayer of brushing Nina, feeling her heartbeat, and having her lips touch my hand as she nibbled treats. I missed celebrating the Holy Eucharist, and I missed sitting deeply in the saddle and feeling the weight of the world drop from my shoulders with each step the horse took. I missed my parishioners on Sunday, and I missed my barn family.

The yearning was not a hole, painfully empty, but a space I could recognize as one where God and I found each other. The boundaries were clearly built by love. Not the sweet, delicate love, but the kind whose posts were deeply embedded in the soil, not easily moved or shaken. The space held, not to be filled by a poor substitute of work like washing windows or binge-watching Netflix.

As the deer longs for the water-brooks, so longs my soul for you, O God. My soul is athirst for God, athirst for the living God; when shall I come to appear before the presence of God?

After six weeks, the hole was filled to overflowing as I clucked Spencer to a trot. All the horses were a bit out of shape. I'd gotten a bit out of shape, too, but the shape where God and horses reside in my soul held strong.

I trotted around the outdoor arena. The sun reflected off the clouds across the paddock next to the arena. For a moment, all of us looked at the beauty of this place, our place, our home.

In the saddle, in the arena with horses whose names and quirks I knew, riding with friends who knew my name and my quirks, I emerged from the cave, the cell, the hermitage of solitude. I had yearned and discovered the foundational place in my relationship with God, and the place that horses have in my soul. While that was painful, the yearning was good for me. And on this almost summer evening, I appeared before God's presence as I sat in the saddle and felt overwhelmed with love that, thankfully, cannot be reduced to anything rational, thankful for the yearning.

CHAPTER 20

Bumps, Bruises, and Broken Bones

Riding a horse is not a gentle hobby, to be picked up and laid down like a game of solitaire. It is a grand passion. It seizes a person whole and once it has done so [they] will have to accept that [their lives] will be radically changed.
—RALPH WALDO EMERSON

S o, what could I have done to stay on?" he asked.

I was sitting in an exam room with Keith. He was lying on a hospital bed with the usual monitors attached to him. His pants, cut off by the nurses, his shoes, socks, and shirt were in a bag next to my chair. I shifted, trying uselessly to find a comfortable position in soaking wet jeans, now semidried to a clammy dampness. I'd rinsed some of the sand out of my socks in the hospital bathroom, but not enough. I was cold, but shaking because of the adrenaline. I'd seen Keith fall off his horse, and then galloped my own horse into the waves, jumped off, and pulled another rider out of the sea, whose horse had gotten spooked.

I think her horse ran back to the beach after she fell off, but I wasn't sure. I just knew I had the reins of the horse I'd been riding in one hand and my friend's arm in another, and I did not think a California beach trail ride at sunset should end like this.

I was still replaying the chaos in my mind, vibrating from the trauma of what had happened and what could have happened. Some friends and I had gone on a retreat, and part of the retreat was a horseback ride on the beach that ended with three of us, including the wrangler leading us, out of the saddle and on the ground. Keith's horseback ride ended with him on the wet sand with as much give as a marble countertop and began a night with doctors fascinated with the way his bones had broken.

I admired his gumption, wanting to know what he could have done to stay on a horse that spooked while he lay partially sedated in a hospital exam room.

I could think of a few things any equestrian can do to stay on a horse, none of which would actually be helpful in this moment. I sighed, shifted in my jeans which were getting unpleasantly cool in the always chilly hospital rooms, and said the thing most equestrians never want to admit.

"Sometimes there's just nothing to do but fall off."

Many times, when the horse turns one way and we go the other, we end up with some bruises, a stiff joint or two, and an extra dose of Advil for a few days. But sometimes, when you ride a horse, you will have *that* fall, the one that breaks a bone (or a few), causes some internal bruising, and makes you rethink your relationship with these magnificent, independent-minded creatures.

As someone who has been in the emergency room bed from a fall and by the bedside of other people who have been injured, I'm here to say that being the one beside the bed is harder, even for a priest who is often by bedsides of people who are sick and even those who are dying.

I want so much for horses to be the enchanted, ethereal experience for everyone that they are for me. I'd hoped that Keith would ride his trail horse down the beach, watch the sunset, and experience God in a new way.

His broken bone was not in my hope.

Perhaps my hope was more of an ideal. If everything had gone just right, then we would have all been energized and renewed by a week of retreat time together, and the sunset beach ride with horses would have been a part of that. We'd probably have even preached on it as a mountaintop experience.

Horses, however, are real. Our relationship with them, however long and intricate and beautiful, is real. And real relationships never follow the ideal. They always lead to some kind of brokenness, hurt, and disappointment. The happily ever after in fairy tales comes only after deep and often horrible brokenness. Our faith deepens in the midst of the places where life breaks us open, when we fall and there's nothing we can do but fall. Sometimes we fall because the forces of life and gravity are greater than our desire to stay upright, and sometimes we're thrown.

Either way, we smash to the ground and suffer the pain.

The word *suffer* comes from the biblical Greek word for passion, as in the passion of Christ. While our modern culture mostly relates passion to deep, amorous love, its origins embrace a profound desire that must be borne. And the birth process is messy and painful.

The Passion accounts in the Gospels relate to Jesus's last hours, which end with his death on the cross. Passion holds the complexity of something that is endured for a greater love.

Passion reminds us that what we love will bruise us, if for nothing else because we will make sacrifices of our passion, for what we love.

In my Episcopal tradition, as well as many other Christian denominations, the Sunday before Easter Sunday is known as The Sunday of the Passion: Palm Sunday. It's a long title to encompass the vastness of the passion of Christ's love for us. It can be a bit jarring. Worshipers begin with celebratory songs and prayers. We wave palms and listen to the account of Jesus riding on a donkey (or two donkeys, according to Matthew, which is some impressive riding by Jesus) as he makes his triumphal entry into Jerusalem. People were so enthusiastic about his arrival they waved branches and shouted, "Hosanna!" a word of adoration and praise.

These people, disciples, friends, those who had heard Jesus preach and even those who were just caught up in the moment, were passionate. Some had heard about Jesus's healing miracles. Many had likely heard his message of vast and inclusive love. His disciples, men and women and people who knew him, shouted in the midst of this passion, this rabbi Jesus who ignited something within them that could only be borne through these shouts of joy and praise.

The liturgy, however, doesn't stay there. We stop, after all the hymns, prayers, and shouts of our own joy, and pray. "Almighty God, whose most dear Son went not up to joy but first he suffered pain, and entered not into glory before he was crucified: Mercifully grant that we, walking in the way of the cross, may find it none other than the way of life and peace; through Jesus Christ our Lord."[10]

We pray again, asking God that we may walk in the way of suffering, and the service moves us into the reading of the

Passion of our Lord Jesus Christ. The reading ends with Jesus, dead on the cross.

That, indeed, devolved quickly.

Some clergy have decided that the two Gospel readings together—the triumphal entry into Jerusalem and the Passion—are too extreme to be read on the same day, in the same worship service. Let Palm Sunday be Palm Sunday, then come back on Good Friday for the Passion Gospel. Decades ago, the Passion Gospel was read the Sunday before, which creates an even stranger flow. I used to argue that same point. Let us shout, "Hosanna!" on Palm Sunday. And stay in that place, at least for a day.

Then I began to be caught in the passion of love, of relationships, and of horses. Passion, I think, means we will suffer and we will sacrifice. Weeping does spend the night, as does pain and hurt. And joy comes in the morning.

Jesus rode into Jerusalem on the back of a donkey, cognizant of what was likely to happen. The complexities and consequences of love were not lost on him. Jesus did not preach a love that made everything okay. He preached a love that was real and messy, that healed those who were broken by life and by prejudices, and that healing made people angry. Jesus welcomed those whom others looked upon with suspicion and judgment. The people my grandmother would have described as being a few sandwiches shy of a picnic. He preached a love that was all-consuming. "Take up your cross and follow me," he says, as I try desperately to figure out how I can take up his cross and still be comfortable all the time.

I can't.

Because Jesus invites us into passion. The cross is heavy at times, and the rough, unfinished wood sends splinters into our skin. When we embrace this passionate love Jesus shares with us, we will be bumped and bruised along the way by the reality of life.

Not always, however. I worry that the ideas of suffering and sacrifice can be twisted so that we think abuse and exploitation are okay. They aren't, although some Christian faiths through the eons have decided that any joy whatsoever means you're not doing this faith right.

Suffering and passion are unified qualities of life and faith. We cannot expect to love without times of heartbreak, disappointment, and hurt. We cannot love without grief. I cannot expect to love horses passionately without some suffering, some bruises and breaks, some disappointments and even some, hopefully rare, times of devastation.

I cannot expect to love humans as God calls me to love without all the same realities.

I want otherwise. I want the myth that the things we love always and only bring us joy and elation, the feeling I have when I've had a confident ride in the show ring and then hear my horse and me announced as the winners.

Yay!

But for every blue ribbon, for every confident ride, there were double and triple that number of rides where I didn't hear my name called, where I felt disappointed at how I'd ridden, and where I'd even, in my suffering, decided I wasn't going to show again. Ever.

My passion for horses gets me through these moments, right back into the saddle, even right back into the show ring.

I'd like the community of the faithful to be without suffering too. As with the feeling I have on horses on our best days, I want the community that promises to love each other with the love God has for us to be without suffering, loss, grief, and disappointment. I want us all to transition seamlessly into new awareness, change, and broader love.

I don't want any of those times when we bump into one another's brokenness and come away with bruises on our souls. I don't want to admit that sometimes, whether riding a horse or being in a relationship, we fall off and hurt ourselves and others, because falling off is the only thing we can do at times.

Real community and real relationships are filled with passion, that emotion and holy call to engage in something that almost overwhelms us because the holy parts of our souls know this is part of faith and love and God.

The church has broken parts of me far more than any falls from horses have. Some horses have been so damaged by their experience with human attempts at training and human neglect that they can only lash out. The same is true for people. We are often so damaged by our experiences and so resistant to help and healing that we lash out at others. Hurt people hurt people, as the saying goes.

Sometimes we just fall off, and those things we love, for which we have a holy passion, will always have an element of suffering. To pretend otherwise isn't real.

CHAPTER 21
Holy Hellfire

※❋❋❋❋❋❋※

*H*orses in the Bible are an embodiment of hellfire, the stomping weapons of war used by the Hittites, the Egyptians, and the Assyrians. The horse made its big entrance into the world of humans not as the mythical creature of companionship or the helpmate to family farms, but as the fierce weapon of war used by humans to subdue and kill other humans.

Horses provided speed that Ancient Near Eastern armies used to encircle and overwhelm their opponents. They crushed enemies underneath their hooves. Art from the era shows warriors riding astride while pulling their arrow in a bow. The archaeological record suggests that riders astride were the first incarnations of war horses, and by 2000 BCE, chariots drawn by horses were the established, essential weapons of war for the civilizations of the Ancient Near East.

This hellfire ferocity was not lost on the writers of biblical texts. Horses get their biggest narrative in the Hebrew testament book of Job, a writing that attempts to understand why an all-powerful God allows tragedy to befall humans. The book begins with a cosmic conversation between God and the *ha'satan* (most accurately translated as the accuser, not Satan, the embodiment of all evil). God points out how faithful Job is, and the accuser suggests, not inaccurately, that perhaps Job, like many humans, is faithful to God because life is going well.

They basically make a cosmic bet. Tragedy befalls Job—his wife and children die, he loses his wealth, and develops some serious skin issues. Near the end of the book, Job, likely in his exhaustion from all that has befallen him and the mostly unhelpful advice from his three friends, challenges God.

"I'm basically a good guy, so what the hell, God?"

And God answers, not in the most tender, compassionate way, but in some ways, the way of a horse. Rearing up on hind legs and snorting hellfire, God answers Job out of the tempest, one of God's favorite ways of showing up to humans. God reminds Job that Job is human and God is God, using several examples of wild animals and one example of a domesticated animal, the horse.

> Do you give the horse its might?
>> Do you clothe its neck with mane?
> Do you make it leap like the locust?
>> Its majestic snorting is terrible.
> It paws violently, exults mightily;
>> it goes out to meet the weapons.
> It laughs at fear, and is not dismayed;
>> it does not turn back from the sword.
> Upon it rattle the quiver,
>> the flashing spear, and the javelin.
> With fierceness and rage it swallows the ground;
>> it cannot stand still at the sound of the trumpet.
> When the trumpet sounds, it says "Aha!"
>> From a distance it smells the battle,
>> the thunder of the captains, and the shouting.
> (Job 39:19–25)

The hellfire of horses continues in the book of Revelation, where horses make several appearances in ways that would not translate well into a Disney movie. The four horsemen of the apocalypse split the heavens and ride into town, probably in another tempest: a white horse with a rider carrying a bow, ready for war; a red horse rending peace from the earth and opening the gaping wound for slaughter; a black horse with a rider carrying scales unleashing famine; and Death riding a pale green horse with Hades following.

Later in the text, more hopeful but no less terrifying images of horses appear:

> Then I saw heaven opened, and there was a white horse! Its rider is called Faithful and True, and in righteousness he judges and makes war. His eyes are like a flame of fire, and on his head are many diadems; and he has a name inscribed that no one knows but himself. He is clothed in a robe dipped in blood, and his name is called The Word of God. (Rev. 19:11–13)

Early Christians continued this message of horses in icons. Saints George and Michael are both riding horses, white and red respectively in ancient art as they plunge their spears into dragons.

The horse in the Bible and in early Christianity does not symbolize a calm and cooperative companion animal. The biblical horse is not Nina, my sweet chestnut mare who calmly teaches children to ride and who daintily tucks her back hooves under her as she naps in her stall.

Still, I admit that I'm attracted to this hellfire heritage of the horse. I'm a Southern woman with a goodly streak of redneck, which means I'm a lot of fun until I'm not. That's a nice way of saying I'm part hellfire, a part of me that I, like many women, had to grow into. Most of my childhood was spent avoiding my hellfire and trying to be nice, to be the unobtrusive good girl.

Being that good girl almost always means holding in all the times you want to tell someone your heart hurts, or that the world feels too much, or crying in your childhood closet because if your parents see your tears, they will simply tell you to quit feeling sorry for yourself.

I've always been intrigued and captivated by people who truly are deeply sweet and nice, those people who embody the spirit of Saint Therese of the Little Flower, who I hold was canonized mainly because she was simply and authentically so kind to everyone she encountered. For far too long, I believed this way was the only way to be like Jesus—the sweet, kindhearted, and benevolent Jesus who is the living water to quench the hellfire in our souls. After all, the church of my childhood emphasized the compliant, obedient Jesus for those who identify as girls and women.

The hellfire Jesus, and yes, it is there, was edited out, except during revivals when the hellfire was waved around by the preacher as a threat of souls' eternal damnation for being too much.

Except that like horses and God, humans have a hellfire streak, a part of our souls that burns with passion and intensity. When we discover our hellfire, the moment is almost seductive, especially if we've been told no one likes an angry woman or the many other ways society and the church tell us we aren't worthy to wield holy hellfire. No doubt if left unchecked or tamped down too long, the embers can burn out, leaving our souls cold and devoid of life. Or it can suddenly combust into a rage that leaves the earth scorched and the person stunned at the flames that came forth.

At the first church I served, a member of the leadership who was utterly opposed to the full welcome and inclusion of LGBTQ+ members told me I needed to sign a statement saying that homosexuality was a sin. Before I really knew what had happened, the hellfire came forth and tables were flipped. Metaphorically, of course, but I was angered enough to flip tables and let my fire burn down the building. I didn't sign any such statement, and I also saw any hope of a relationship with that member left in ashes. And honestly, I was fine with that. Such is a consequence of that part of our souls, when we allow this holy hellfire to burn. We might be left with ashes, which could be the beginning of renewal and reconciliation.

Or we could just look at the ashes and shrug our shoulders at the mess, figuring someone else will clean it up.

I chose door number two, and still am okay with that choice. I also realize that choice is not exactly the model option of loving my neighbors or my enemies. Eventually, my part of the mess will be mine to resolve . . . eventually.

Such is the nature of holy hellfire, which reminds me hellfire ought to scare us in that fear of the Lord way. Hellfire is a holy part of my soul that stirs up zealousness for love and justice. Hellfire spurns us to march, to kneel, and speak truth to power. It kindles the embers in us to let us know something is wrong, an anger that smolders and invites us to sit in its glow of discernment until we are warmed enough to act. Hellfire purged the lips of the prophets so they spoke hard truths to

God's people who were ignoring the call to love. It fell upon the heads of the disciples at Pentecost, creating such a ruckus that bystanders asked if the followers of Jesus were drunk and moving these same followers to venture out into the vastness and diverseness of humanity to preach love.

Hellfire in our souls, like hellfire horses, demands our respect and our fearful veneration. It is a holy power that, when used judiciously and tempered with love, can shift the arc of society toward justice. Used recklessly and allowed to burn wild, we wield a power that can decimate.

Too often, instead of letting the presence of holy hellfire humble and even unsettle us, so that we recognize and honor it, we want to justify our destructive flames and quench and conquer the flames in others. Fire uses up so much oxygen, and when ours burns out of control, there is no breathing space in the room for others.

We meet hellfire with hellfire, until there is no breath left in any of us.

Riders are attracted to hellfire horses, those that are not especially interested in a human-horse partnership but would rather buck and kick and tell us to stay away. All horses, like all humans, buck and kick on occasion, especially when we are learning something new in partnership with each other. But some horses are what I call hellfire horses, simply happy to not be ridden and better off living life on their terms.

War Emblem was a hellfire horse. He won both the Preakness and the Kentucky Derby in 2002. I met him at Old Friends Equine Retirement in Georgetown, Kentucky, not far from my home. I listened to the guide explain why War Emblem had a double-fenced paddock.

"He bites . . . everyone, and he really just wants to be left alone."

She explained how one day, War Emblem, who had a successful career as a racehorse, simply stopped running during a training session.

Stopped. Cold. And no amount of prodding or coaching could get him to run anymore.

They sent him to stud, first in the United States and then in Japan, which he had no interest in doing. He did sire some foals, but apparently his hellfire attitude almost killed several of his handlers during that time. She said that when he was loaded on the plane to fly back to the United States, his handlers cheered when he officially left Japanese airspace. He resided at Old Friends until he died a few years ago, happy to have been left alone with human and horse neighbors a double fence away.

During the early morning tour when I met him, I watched him run in his paddock at hellfire speed. Here was the horse of God in Job, the horse of Revelation, the horse that can be witnessed from a distance, but not conquered by us. Not even a horse to be fed a treat by us.

"He'd take the treat, then probably bite you," the docent confirmed.

We riders can become enamored with conquering horses as a way to prove our skill as riders, as if conquering is of higher value than developing a cooperative relationship of mutual respect.

I've never ridden a truly hellfire horse like War Emblem, nor do I plan to do so. I've ridden horses that I considered hellfire at the time, and I also know my instructor Stephanie would never risk my well-being with such a horse. But

I understand the desire and have had it myself, to ride something that big and even dangerous. In my early years, I wanted to ride the difficult horses to prove . . . something.

But being a good rider isn't about conquering hellfire or horses. And being a faithful Christian isn't about conquering either. Both are about relationships, and using the tools we have to build them, strengthen them, challenge them when needed, and even to reconcile them.

I've found that when I have a horse who is living in the neighborhood of hellfire, I don't ride her by spewing forth flames myself. I find my own calm and centeredness. I listen to what she is telling me by her snorting and pulling and even bucking. Steph likes to remind me, when I can feel my frustration rising with a horse who's being challenging, not to get in a fight with the horse.

She's right.

So I talk, calmly, more to myself than the horse, but that bit of holy peace almost always works. Not a compliant peace, but a peace that is enflamed by a passion for the relationship I have with horses, all of who they are. I get quiet and listen to what they are telling me about themselves and about my riding.

Am I pulling too much on the reins, and she wants me to loosen? Am I being vague about what I want, saying I want her to trot but not giving her enough slack to move forward? Am I in a hellfire space because of the day or the week I've had? Is she frightened of something she sees that I need to assure her is okay?

Long ago, horses moved beyond being only creatures of war in our imaginations. Through the centuries they became the partner of humans to plow ground to plant crops, to move across land, and simply to enjoy an afternoon ride. But when I ride, even the ones who are kind and sweet, I'm always aware of the hellfire legacy. As I tell kids who walk behind horses and do things in the barn that discount back hooves, there are good reasons why you should never do that.

Hellfire is almost always an invitation to listen—to the other, to ourselves, and to God.

CHAPTER 22

I Hold Things

*H*olding things doesn't come with detailed instructions or reflective books we can read and discuss in small groups. We come into the world knowing we need to hold things and learning how to hold things. It's not brain surgery. It's simply holding things.

Babies hold the fingers of their parents. Children hold the hands of an adult as they are in a busy, crowded place. I hold reins as I ride and hold the paten as I distribute the body of Christ to people. I hold the hands of little boys who are being baptized who aren't sure they will be able to walk up the step stool by themselves. I hold the hands of people in prayer circles as we gather for holy time. I hold the hands of precious ladies as they have yet another needle stick for a medical test that will hurt, but we talk about the weather or weekly trips to the beauty parlor instead. I hold the hands of those who are making their final great journey until they let go and take the hands of God who is waiting for them just beyond the place we can see from this side of the kingdom.

I hold anger and pain. Often, life is too much . . . too hard, too hurtful, too sad, too horrible . . . for one person to hold all of those feelings. So we share our heartaches and gashes of our souls. And we hold some of that pain for the other. We don't fix it or redeem it or give meaning to it. Nope. We just hold it for a while.

I even hold joy—those amazing moments of laughter and delight, when new life and light bursts forth. Shield the joyous, we pray. I do by holding some of it as well. Like the effervescence of life overflowing, we get showered by that joy. Hold on to that when it comes your way.

I hold silence. Life is noisy, and it is also silent. We seem to be profoundly good at adding words to the world, but holding silence is a bit harder. I hold that too: quiet, still silence to allow for the sighs too deep for words to have their place.

I hold people in their pain and grief. I hold them if they need to be held and cry. If they don't want to be held, I hold myself in that place and just sit with them. And they cry. I cry, too, at times. Sometimes I've wondered if someone would ever stop crying, or if I would ever stop crying. I hold tissues as they gather the tears. Again, I don't fix anything. I just hold.

I even hold a fair amount of crazy. We all do. We hold each other's eccentricities and outbursts over minor things because the major things are simply too scary to face.

When we love others, when we serve and care, we hold. Holding doesn't provide lofty answers or intricate theology. It just offers presence and hands to share the weight of whatever burden we may be feeling. Holding isn't complicated or big. It is intimate and small, offering one of the simplest acts of humanity—babies hold, children hold. Children of God hold, if even for a short time.

But I need things held as well. We can forget that when we are holding another's things. Then one day, we feel overwhelmed, weighted down, and crushed underneath all the things.

So where do I put them?

Perhaps one of the great gifts my horse, Nina, gives me is that for all the holding I do in my life, when I ride, she reminds me that I can't hold everything all the time. So she says, "Hop up, Mom, and let me hold you for a while as we ride." She holds me in her unique and elegant way. I hold the reins to guide her. She, after all, is very good at making me feel useful in this way.

We walk, and I look at the world through her ears, two fuzzy, expressive guides that remind me to focus on what's in front of me and not be quite so distracted by all the periphery, even if only for an hour or so. We trot, and she holds me as I sit up and back, opening my chest and shoulders, which are often tight and crunched from worry and stress. Open up, her gait tells me. Breathe deeply and ride.

We canter, and she holds me as I sit deeply in her beautiful easy canter that rhythmically massages my lower back with each stride, rolling and stretching the muscles that too often hold tension and pain. I sit deep and quiet, and for these few moments, feel her movement unlock the tension in my back and free my soul to fly.

She holds me, my joy, my grief, my disappointments, and my excitement. She holds all of my soul, carefully and with grace and strength, the way God holds me.

In all these ways, Nina holds me so that when I need to hold something again, I'm ready.

Of all the things we do, perhaps our ability to hold things is one of the purest incarnations of love, for humans and horses.

CHAPTER 23
Being Seen

❊

Love consists in this, that two solitudes
protect and touch and greet each other.
—RAINER MARIA RILKE, *LETTERS TO A YOUNG POET*

*T*he entire body of a horse is as sensitive to touch as our human fingertips. Nina can feel a fly land on a hair in her tail, resulting in a quick swish to suggest it land elsewhere. A miniscule movement of my fingers on the reins of horses with sensitive mouths communicates a halt or a move to one side or the other. A slight shift in the saddle as I drop my hips deeper asks the horse to slow just a bit. When I press my right leg into the side of a horse, they will shift left, away from the pressure.

Touch is important with any horse. Their heightened sensitivity means they feel things in ways we can easily overlook. This equine sensitivity allows a rider to communicate with slight movements, even movements so slight we may not realize we are making them. To slow a canter, I can often simply sit up slightly. Saying nothing while I allow my body to sit straighter in the saddle communicates a confidence to the horse, almost always resulting in a more collected canter. The horse's exquisite ability to notice touch means a horse feels my presence. "I notice you. I feel your presence. I feel you," their bodies tell me when I ride.

Horses pair this extraordinary skin sensitivity with their eyes. Horses have the largest eyes of any mammal on land. They watch the world with those large, luminous eyes. They seem to have the capacity to see separately, each eye taking in distinct images that are processed by their brains in ways we don't completely understand. When I walk into a stall with a mare and her new foal, they both watch me. They make eye contact with me, part of their assessment of who I am. Do I mean harm to her baby? Do I have food? I notice you. I see you.

Do I see them? Do I feel them?

Too often, I don't, these 1,000-pound creatures of God. I often come to the barn after a day of one too many meetings and I have one too many feelings. I'm a bit frazzled, sometimes rushed, the world of my life, the big concerns have left a dull throb from the sting and the little things fly around my soul like gnats, being bothersome and stealing my focus. In my early riding days, I would fly into the barn on two wheels. If the horse I was riding wasn't ready, I'd grab a bridle and bridle them, taking a few moments to rub them and say a passing, "Hello."

My touch was frantic. My spirit was frenzied. I didn't take time to let the horse see me, and I certainly didn't take the time to see the horse. When I do this, this not seeing, not noticing, my rides usually start with more nervous energy than either the horse or I need. I'm tight. The horse feels my tension and translates that feeling into anxiety. If she's nervous, then surely there's something I should be nervous about, the horse thinks. We don't flat walk, and the speed of our other gaits is often faster than it should be. When I don't notice, don't touch, don't see this creature with whom I'm in relationship, the relationship isn't at its fullest. When I don't give the horse time to notice, touch, and see me, they don't have full trust in me.

Relationship is a yearning, in some ways, of all God's creatures. Humans yearn for and need relationship. Like horses, we are wired for community. Community and relationships come in all shapes and sizes, but the ones our souls yearn for are those where we are truly and fully known, seen, and noticed: our joys and sorrows, our stellar qualities and our questionable ones, our quirks and our downright seedy underbelly.

They are all known. And in a holy, miraculous way, they are loved.

We are felt. We are noticed. We are seen.

To do that, however, means we have to return the favor. Relationships are not one-way streets, or the ones where we are known and loved are not one-way streets. I have to take the time to let another notice me and see me. To have this deep relationship with horses, I have to take the time.

Horses I've known and ridden for years know me. Using all their marvelous senses, they identify me quickly, but I still take time for nuzzles and the occasional smear of slobber as they smell, touch, and see me.

New horses need more time with me. And I need more time with them. My riding reminds me that the time on the ground with a horse, being felt, seen, and noticed, is as important as the time I spend in the saddle. These moments are us asking the questions that may take several rides to answer.

Who are you? How do you like to be touched? Will you look at me in the eyes and see me? Will you let me see you? Will you take the time to learn about me? Will you let me learn about you?

I thought about these questions as I met Sancho.

But barely.

Today I was having trouble being noticed and being seen. The day had been particularly harried. I was running late to the barn. Traffic, of course, was heavier than usual, which made me even later. My soul was not stilled.

I walked into the barn to discover I was riding Sancho. I'd never ridden him before. Sancho is a five-year-old gelding who is transitioning into the lesson program. And on this day, this hectic day where my feelings were running all over my skin in this emotional slurry, I was riding him for the first time.

I felt my anxiety rise. I'd really wanted one of the horses that needed a strong presence to ride, one that I had a long-term relationship with. I could just slip into the saddle and be known and seen because we had a past. Instead, I was riding a horse that was almost completely unknown to me. I'd seen others ride him, and I knew he needed a calm confidence to ride, as most young horses do. A few years ago, I would have believed I couldn't ride Sancho after my day. Even after several years of riding, on this day, I heard that whisper.

"You aren't really a good rider. You can't ride him."

I heard that voice, blended with my emotions. I've heard that voice before. But I was tired on this day, so it resonated stronger than usual.

In response, I reached out and touched Sancho's neck. He leaned into my touch. I stood there, present with him, present to his touch as he was present to mine. His neck was thick with his winter coat that hadn't begun to shed. It felt strong and sturdy, and much of his mane hair stood straight up like an almost-too-long Mohawk. His warmth eased into my fingers, achy and tired from work. His smell, strong of fresh grass from the fields, brought me fully into the barn and into his presence.

We looked at each other. His eyes are a deep brown, the color of my coffee that I'd left on the counter by accident as I rushed out this morning. The beautiful brown filled the space—no white showing. A calm horse usually doesn't show the white sclera. Sancho saw me, looked at me, with the largest eyes I would ever see on the earth. I could see the exquisite holy darkness in them. His eyes are framed by reddish-brown lashes with flecks of white hairs. They saw me with a depth perhaps matched only by the way God sees. They invited me to stop, to be, and see him with an openness and exposure rarely shared between humans seeing each other for the first time.

The world, with all its frantic movement, retreated as we saw each other. And in that moment, I knew I could ride. I knew he would let me ride him.

Not that our ride would be flawless. What I knew is that we had noticed, touched, and seen each other and the relationship could begin. I've ridden some of the horses in the barn hundreds of times. This was my first ride on Sancho. We were starting our partnership together.

I stepped up on the mounting block and put my left foot in the stirrup. Swinging my right leg over and into the stirrup, I took some more breaths and clucked him to a walk. Steph, ever the observant instructor, reminded me that he was a good boy, and he's learning. I reminded myself Steph would never put me on a horse I couldn't ride.

"Don't overthink it," she added, as she often does, knowing me well. My first couple of trips around the arena on Sancho were tighter for me. I could notice that. He could notice that. I breathed and looked through his ears.

I clucked him into a trot, and I let touch and feel do their magic. I felt him move, and he felt me move. I let the reins slack to see how he'd respond. I rolled my knees in to get a firmer seat, which in slight contradiction, actually relaxed me. The outdoor arena still had patches of mud from a rainstorm earlier in the day. Because of the patches, Steph had us stopping and walking around the main muddy corner, then picking up the trot when we'd cleared the mud. Sancho needed a bit of a longer runway to shift from a trot to a flat walk, and he needed me to post to the end and not fall forward.

He needed to feel my touch of confidence, which gave him his own confidence. Two passes and Sancho figured out this new game. Smart horse, I noticed. Plus, he needed me to talk to him, calmly, sweetly. Not what my spirit was feeling when I arrived, but what Sancho and I needed. He needed my calm, and I needed his.

My lesson on Sancho was a witness to the grounding, holy power of touch and of taking the time to notice and to see. I could have rushed into the saddle, firmly telling myself that I could ride him and denying how messy I was feeling. I could have not stopped to see him or, as important, to let him see me. Sancho didn't know me from Adam's housecat an hour ago. Now he does.

In all our advancement, we often forget the deep, holy power of touch, of being noticed, of being seen, and of being known. Horses have not forgotten the holy power of those things.

When he and I were done that day, I brushed Sancho down and rubbed him with a towel. He'd worked hard, calming me, centering me, and being an all-around wonderful ride. His teddy-bear fur was damp where the saddle and girth had held in the sweat. After I rubbed him on his back and withers for several minutes, he turned his head back and nudged my hand with the towel. He looked at me again with those striking coffee eyes.

"You want your face rubbed?" I asked. He did. Every horse loves a good touch that they will tell you about when you let them. Nina has a particular place on her neck that is her favorite place to be scratched. She will tilt and lean her head into my fingers as I snuggle her. Noah likes his ears rubbed, and he will lower it to my hand as I'm removing his tack, his way of reminding me that he expects pets. I added Sancho's face to the list.

I give him one final, hefty rub.

This is what I know for sure: the love of God that we are all called into consists of noticing each other, touching each other, when we welcome that holy context, and seeing each other with careful attention. This is holy relationship, being known and loved.

Being noticed.

Being seen.

CHAPTER 24
Domestication

*I*t is an astonishing story how horses and humans found each other. The ancestor of the horse, like most mammal ancestors, didn't look much like our modern *Equus*. *Hyracotherium*—which looked more like Evie, my Jack Russell terrier mix, than Nina, my horse—appeared on earth some 60 million years ago. It had five toes that had not yet evolved into the one toe we know as a hoof. Then, about 17 million years ago, the first recognizable sort-of horse appeared in *Merychippus*. Time marched on, the grasslands shifted to forests and back again, and *Equus* finally appeared some 4 million years ago.

Horses as we know them existed in the Americas, but for reasons debated by scientists, died out in this geographical region about 8,000 BCE. They remained in Eurasia, but their numbers dwindled until 6,000 years ago. Scientists originally thought horses were first domesticated by the Botai people, who lived on grasslands in northern Kazakhstan. But recent DNA analysis shows the horse domesticated by the Botai is a relative of the Przewalski's horse, which is related to, but not the same, as *Equus*. Further, our modern Przewalski's horse is truly wild, not domesticated.

The current theory is that horses were domesticated in Persia. Others think there was not a single domestication event, but several across various cultures where horses and humans intermingled. Whatever the fossil record reveals, what is known is that domestication saved the beloved horse from extinction, and may well have saved humans as well. So today, horses are domesticated, all of them. Horses commonly called wild are not wild. They are feral.

Because of horses, we had a partner in agriculture, in hunting, and in forming what would eventually be settled communities. All this, in some way, through the miracle of domestication.

Domestication is a term that seems to have some fluidity in meaning. Fundamentally it means adapting plants and animals for human use by selective breeding. Who, I wondered, does the adapting?

"We don't really know," Dr. Ernie Bailey said. "There are likely several genetic components involved that makes an animal like the horse predisposed to domestication." Dr. Bailey is an equine geneticist at the University of Kentucky who good-naturedly answered my many questions about how humans and horses came to this point of relationship.

Of thousands of species of mammals, fewer than twenty are domesticated. The numbers suggest domestication is a very rare event, and not solely a matter of human will. Horses, after all, are domesticated. But their close relatives the zebras? Nope.

We've tried to domesticate zebras. And failed spectacularly. While all equines bite or threaten to bite as a way of warning and protection, horses will nip and let go to convey their message of "Back off." Zebras are aggressive biters who hang on once locked. They go for blood. That has, obviously, not worked well for zebra-human relationships.

Dr. Bailey offered that some working theories of why some animals and not others have partnered with humans in domestication include an adaptable diet that allowed animals to survive eating a wide variety of things as they followed nomadic humans moving from locale to locale or stayed near humans who had settled in communities (horses likely really enjoyed eating the crops humans planted, and discovered the easy dinner was worth the human annoyances that came with it); and prolific breeding in captivity (not all animals breed easily or at all in captivity—think giant pandas). Other suggestions have to do with temperament, panic response, quick maturation, and a social structure that includes living in herds, a hierarchy within the herd, and general but not exclusive habitats.

With all these factors that have to come together, I'm willing to explain domestication as a holy mystery, which makes not only the domestication but the sheer survival of horses because of domestication miraculous and certainly holy.

Because it is relational. Horses found humans beneficial, and humans certainly found horses beneficial. But beyond the functionality, horses and humans thrived together. We chose each other because we thrived in relationship with each other.

Wildness, for all its romantic notions, is a hard life. Ernie recalled a story of a scarred and worn lion he'd seen on a research trip who was head of his pride and who was eventually killed by a younger male. In the wild, survival is foremost. Flourishing is a secondary aspect.

Domestication provides stability, even comfort and flourishing. Domestication offers order. God, in some ways, domesticates the wildness of the *tehon,* the chaos, when God creates the heavens and earth and all that is in it in Genesis. God, in one creation account, is a force of order in the chaos that exists before.

Then humans enter the picture and live in Eden, which seems to be that holy place that is neither wild nor domesticated, but in union with God. That comes with a condition, that humans simply could not handle.

Seriously, we had one job—not to eat the fruit of one tree.

Which we failed, and that resulted in our entering into wildness, a severe world where death and sin were with us, and where our energy seemed to be consumed with sheer survival in the midst of harshness. God kept offering us a way to flourish through relationship, but not surprisingly, we decided mostly to do our own thing. The idea of being domesticated was not palatable, perhaps.

Until what I consider our domestication event with God through Abraham, Sarah, and Hagar. God offered us relationship, one that benefited us—again. There were rules— love God, love your neighbor, and love yourself. Don't bite each other and hang on. And we humans agreed. The holiness of domestication of humans brought us into relationship with God and God in relationship with us.

I suspect seeing our relationship with God as one of domestication is not a comforting description, especially with our human fantasy of wildness. The idea that we could survive and thrive in the wild is the stuff of deeply edited reality shows and slanted mythology. The reality looks so much more tragic. Wild, for humans, is cast out, alone, and dispossessed. God is certainly there, in the places where we have cast out the humans in need of refuge and shelter and kindness.

Domestication is a shift, a move into flourishing, into relationship.

Horses have given me a new and holy appreciation for domestication. That Nina's ancestor thousands of years ago saw something in a human worth investigating and then found something worthwhile in us to create a long-term relationship reflects the moment God created humans and saw everything God created, including humans, and pronounced it very good.

Nina's eyes see me the way God sees me—as a human worthy of relationship, trust, and love. Domestication, perhaps, is rare because this trinity of bond is rare, or at least rarer than it should be. When I ride Nina in our particular relationship, and when I ride any of the horses that move me, I may feel like I'm touching wildness. I may have images of ripping across a field in wild abandon, at times. But what truly moves my soul into a place of trust and love is an astonishing miracle of relationship, of the *we* that is horse and rider, of God and humans, and of Nina and me.

The choices our ancestors made thousands of years ago created the relationship where I canter Nina bareback and feel the freedom that is the holiness of us together. This relationship lets me trot into the show ring on Maria on a perfect September evening and feel the spirit of God wash over us in the fall breeze, and for our moments in the ring, trusting each other to be our best together. This relationship allows the moments when I lean into Nina and kiss the tiny white spot on her nose, and we simply stand, awash in thousands of years of love.

God, the great I AM, loves us, in relationship. God gathers us in the holiness of community, in the miracle of *we*. We were truly not meant to be alone, neither horses nor humans.

Because we were created for this.

CONCLUSION

I started riding at Wingswept Farm by chance.

I originally began riding at another barn, which suddenly ended its lesson program. My then-instructor took me to Wingswept to meet Stephanie and tour the farm a few days before I left to serve as a chaplain at a summer camp. I thought I'd be able to go to one or two other barns and decide, not that I knew exactly what factors I'd be using to decide. After all, I'd never switched horse barns before.

Then, at camp, I received the text message, "We moved Nina to Wingswept today. You can start riding there next week."

Oh. Okay.

I was in the mountains of Eastern Kentucky at the Episcopal Church's camp. It's tucked in the space between mountains, in what we in Appalachia call a holler. And the cell phone reception is terrible on a good day. There is one place near the top of a ridge where cell phone reception is almost guaranteed, but it's a good thirty-minute hike to get there, then a climb that involves a few ropes.

I was not on the top of the ridge when I got the text. I was actually sitting outside in the early morning watching the mist slip away between the trees with the sunrise. In my years as a camp chaplain, I've learned that early morning is the only guaranteed quiet time when young people are around.

I was surprised the text made it through. But it did. And I sat there, at daybreak in the mountains, wondering how long this change would feel weird. Changing barns meant I didn't know where the bridles were kept, or any of the horses. I would also be leaving the horses who initially taught me to ride saddle seat. Changing barns meant a loss, and this loss made me feel unsteady.

I ride Saddlebreds by chance too.

I'd never heard of saddle seat riding until I picked a Groupon out of a list of opportunities to ride. I'd never seen a cutback saddle or held reins that attached to a full bridle and bit or even slow gaited and racked a horse. I just knew I needed a change from the constancy of being a priest and having a life that began and ended in the church. I knew I needed a change to add something that got me outside myself.

In the midst of chance and change, I found American Saddlebred horses and a barn that is as comfortable as a trail ride on Nina in perfect spring weather. I can roll my shoulders back and feel the tension release with every step.

I even have Nina by chance.

I'd never bought a horse before and really had no idea what I was doing. My then-instructor said she was a good horse, and the price was fair, so that was my standard.

I felt overwhelmed when I first rode her, in the same way I've felt overwhelmed when I stand barefooted and exposed in the presence of holiness. The very human part of me that has been strained and punched by sin tells me I shouldn't be here, that I am not worthy to be on such holy ground. Yet God calls me there. God calls all of us there.

It happened one day when I was walking Ivy around the arena. Ivy was new to our lesson program and needed a few miles under saddle to smooth out her trot. She liked to go and could get a bit excited when she trotted. Those are wonderful traits, but the beginner riders that were going to ride her needed her to go a bit slower.

I met Ivy during a lunge lesson. She got upset at a loud noise and I wasn't holding the reins as part of the workout. I learned the value of a good seat and grabbing the mane to stay on. Lauren, a fellow rider at Wingswept, was walking through the arena. Seeing Ivy have a moment, Lauren, nonplussed, said simply, "Good job. That's why you sit deep."

Ivy and I continued our lesson, which was a lesson for both of us in finding calm as we rode—her from the noise and me from the sudden shock to my system that is riding without reins when I really needed them. "That lesson was as good for her as it was for you," Lauren noted later, as we were both putting up tack from our respective rides.

"Maybe I should ride her more to train her," I said, mostly joking.

Lauren wasn't when she said, "That's a good idea. She needs time under saddle."

Another change and chance. For years, horses taught me. Now, I was returning the favor, at least to Ivy. Ivy is a Quarter Horse appendix, meaning she has Thoroughbred in her. She carries her head with that lovely level line that Quarter Horses do, and she's a muscular mare with downy ears that usually have some amount of mud on them from rolling in the stuff in her field.

As we walked around the arena, both of us cooling down after our work, I watched Nina through Ivy's muddy ears. Nina had a small child on her back, probably about seven, who was learning how to canter. The child was trying hard to give Nina her cues to canter. But it's a lot to remember—gently raise one rein to tip Nina's head to the outside rail; put your leg on her; and kiss and say "canter"—especially when the seven-year-old was probably nervous. She was pulling Nina's reins in all sorts of ways, telling Nina to do things with her words that didn't coordinate with her actions.

Nina stood with kind patience, not shaking her head or galloping off. She simply stood, waiting for the little rider to finally figure all the motions out. The child eventually did, mostly, and I watched Nina, exercising the grace of good enough, step off into a perfect canter.

I felt that feeling that I'm not worthy to be part of the holy ground that is Nina. Yet I am, by chance, through changes, and by grace.

God works in the midst of chance, that randomness that infuses human life, when things happen that surprise us, that unseat us from our plans. For me, I'm comforted by this aspect of God, that God doesn't need the world to work in perfect order. Instead, chaos and chances provide pathways into newness. And those are held together by the threads of grace, that holy love we don't earn, but often find ourselves immersed in through no real doing on our part.

And this grace provides change.

Horses have changed me. My barn family has changed me. Nina has changed me. For all the love I have for stability, for the sure and certainness of God, horses have given me a deep and abiding appreciation for the holiness of change. Not because what was before was less than or bad, but that change shifts us into something else. The change expands me and my capacity of love.

I've had Nina now for almost a decade. She's in her early twenties, and two years ago we retired her from showing. Her soundness, which is a general term for a horse's overall health, is appropriate for her age as a senior horse. Her bones, joints, and muscles take a bit longer to warm up, and as a firmly in middle-age woman myself, I completely understand. Her lessons are mostly little ones now, and she adores her job of gently carrying them around the arena as they learn to post a trot and sit a canter. They also give her peppermints.

She and Darcy, another senior mare, enjoy their mornings in one of the fields, grazing and enjoying the world.

I still ride her on the trail and strip off the saddle the little ones ride in after she's had an easy lesson and ride her bareback around the arena. More than not, I realize the amazing grace that brought her into my life.

I do not deserve to sit on the holy ground that is Nina.

And yet love isn't about deserving or earning. Love, as God and Nina and a whole host of horses have shown me, is about the willingness to open myself to it and welcome it, with all its strangeness and unexpectedness. This grace that falls on us like a gentle spring rain changes me, changes us. Because of horses, I've changed as a rider. Because of horses, I've changed as a person of faith.

Horses do that, if we let them. They change us, if we give them the chance.

I've learned to let the relationship between horses and me and between horses and my faith be multidirectional. They all inform each other in creative and even chaotic ways. I find a new confidence in pastoral care and leadership because I ride some sassy, salty horses. I also find confidence in the saddle because I am a priest.

We pray at Compline, the service before we retire for the day: "Be present, O merciful God, and protect us through the hours of this night, so that we who are wearied by the changes and chances of this life may rest in your eternal changelessness; through Jesus Christ our Lord. Amen."[11]

Horses have invited me to see the joy and energy that comes from changes and chances. Not always, but often, I can see how changes and chances have led me to this place of grace, of God, and of horses. I do not deserve it, but I am so thankful I am here.

ACKNOWLEDGMENTS

Writing a book while running a church and being human in the midst of a global pandemic was not on my list. And yet, I did. My world got very small for months, as my human-to-human contact was significantly limited while I watched the tragedy of millions of humans die from COVID-19.

I say with certainty that God and horses kept my soul whole during this time. When I couldn't hug another human, every lesson horse at Wingswept Farm stood ready for my hugs. When the word came that six feet apart was a safe distance, horses not only provided a good visual for me to use to judge that distance between others and me, they also moved right through it to allow me to stand face-to-face with them and be in the intimate space of another being filled with love and life. My daily prayers include a passionate thanks to God for guiding me back to horses almost a decade ago and endless gratitude for the horses at Wingswept who continue to teach me about love, life, and faith.

So as always, I share my abiding love and gratitude for Wingswept Farm, the horses and the humans. Stephanie and Chris Brannan, owners and trainers, and their son Hunter, master trainer, are truly gifts to me and to so many. Again, any errors or incorrect statements about riding or horses are mine alone. Thank you to Alyssa and Lauren, who also encourage me, push me, and make me laugh. Your teaching and your friendship have made me a better rider and a better person.

To my barn family, especially the Wednesday Night Riders, I love you all. To be known and loved is a gift. To ride horses with those who know and love you is valued at a price above rubies.

Wingswept Farm is truly holy ground because love is so present in so many ways.

Thank you also to St. Michael the Archangel Episcopal Church. Your capacity to be creative and to love inspires me. Thank you for knowing my time at the barn is holy time and encouraging me to go to the place where I can come back to myself. Thank you for knowing me and loving me.

Thanks to Paraclete Press for asking if I had another book about horses in me. I didn't know I did. Thank you to my initial editor Jon Sweeney for strongly suggesting I start the book with a chapter about horses, which allowed the grace for the other chapters and eventually this book to be written. I'm so grateful to be part of your publishing family.

Thank you to all who read *Horses Speak of God* and shared it with your friends and fellow horse-loving readers. Writing is a very solitary endeavor, filled with doubt and worry that the words I'm writing won't matter. In the moments where I wanted to hit *delete* on everything, I would receive a note, e-mail, or message via social media (even a few phone calls) where you shared your own love for horses and the many ways they bless our lives and your gratitude for the words of the book. Thank you for your encouragement, your support, your love of reading, your love of God, and your love of horses.

Thank you to my little rescue pup, Evie, who in the six weeks I couldn't ride, was elated that we walked. And walked. And walked. During these walks, I first heard the sentences and phrases that expanded into many of these essays. Writing, it seems, is fashioned by walking. And yes, we still walk, because we do, indeed, find the way by walking. And Evie has to inspect all the neighborhood smells.

I am deeply grateful for my friends and family who put up with having a writer among them. Special thanks to Brad and Elise, for more reasons than I can name.

Thanks to all who love horses, who care for them, rescue them, breed them, train them, show them, and ensure they continue to be part of our world. Thank you especially to all who love American Saddlebreds. On many days, I don't think humans deserve horses, but I'm so thankful they chose us.

And thank you to Nina, for being all the horse I will never deserve, and by whom I am eternally blessed.

NOTES

1 Wendell Berry, *The Unforeseen Wilderness: Kentucky's Red River Gorge* as quoted in *To Be at Peace with Our Essential Loneliness* by Parker J. Palmer, https://onbeing.org/blog/parker-palmer -to-be-at-peace-with-our-essential-loneliness/.

2 The Order of St. Helena, *The Saint Helena Psalter* (New York: Church Publishing, Incorporated 2004), 92. Used by permission.

3 Joan D. Chittister, O.S.B. *The Rule of Benedict: Insights of the Ages* (New York: The Crossroads Publishing Company 1992), 90.

4 L. M. Montgomery, *Anne of Green Gables* (Public Domain at https://www.gutenberg.org/ebooks/45).

5 Episcopal Church. *The Book of Common Prayer and Administration of the Sacraments and Other Rites and Ceremonies of the Church* (New York: The Church Hymnal Corporation 1979), 832.

6 Episcopal Church. *Enriching Our Worship 1* (New York: The Church Pension Fund 1998), 35

7 Abraham Joshua Heschel. *The Sabbath.* (New York: Farrar, Straus and Giroux, 1951), 3.

8 *Book of Common Prayer*, 858.

9 Julian of Norwich, *Showings*, translated from the critical text with an introduction by Edmund Colledge, O.S.A. and James Walsh, S.J. (New Jersey: Paulist Press 1978), 193.

10 *Book of Common Prayer*, 272.

11 *Book of Common Prayer*, 133.

ABOUT PARACLETE PRESS

PARACLETE PRESS is the publishing arm of the Cape Cod Benedictine community, the Community of Jesus. Presenting a full expression of Christian belief and practice, we reflect the ecumenical charism of the Community and its dedication to sacred music, the fine arts, and the written word.

Learn more about us at our website:
www.paracletepress.com
or phone us toll-free at 1.800.451.5006

SCAN
TO
READ
MORE

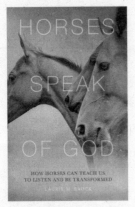